VINTAGE **DIDION**

Joan Didion was born in Sacramento on December 5, 1934. She graduated from the University of California, Berkeley, in 1956 and began working for *Vogue*. For many years her essays and reporting appeared in *The Saturday Evening Post, Esquire,* and *New West.* In 1963 Didion made her fictional debut with *Run River,* a novel about a hop grower's wife in the Sacramento Valley. Over the course of her career, Didion has published four other novels. Her second work of fiction, *Play It As It Lays* (1970), follows a young woman through Hollywood and Las Vegas in the late 1960s, while *A Book of Common Prayer* (1977) inter-twines the stories of two American women in a fictional Central American country. In 1984 she completed *Democracy,* a darkly comic novel set in Hawaii and Southeast Asia at the end of the Vietnam War. Her most recent work of fiction, *The Last Thing He Wanted* (1996), traces a thrilling narrative of discovery and conspiracy.

Didion's first volume of nonfiction, *Slouching Towards Bethlehem,* was published in 1968 to overwhelming critical acclaim. This collection of essays captures the spirit of America in the 1960s, focusing on the counterculture of California. In 1979 Didion published her second collection, *The White Album,* which included reflections on the Manson murders, the Black Panthers, and Georgia O'Keeffe. In the 1980s Didion wrote two studies on United States foreign policy in Central America. These pieces were published together in 1983 as *Salvador,* which is still regarded as one of the most important works of American political reporting. *Miami* (1987) makes the connection between the Cuban exile community and Washington, while both *After Henry* (1992) and *Political Fictions* (2001) deconstruct American culture and the political process. Her most recent book, *Where I Was From,* is about California, about America, about her history and ours and about the contradictions in the stories we tell ourselves about our past and our present.

With her husband, John Gregory Dunne, Didion has cowritten screenplays for several movies including *The Panic in Needle Park, Play It As It Lays, A Star Is Born, True Confessions, Broken Trust,* and *Up Close and Personal.* A contributor to *The New York Review of Books* and *The New Yorker,* she lives in New York City.

VINTAGE DIDION

Joan Didion

VINTAGE BOOKS

A Division of Random House, Inc.

New York

The Library of Congress Cataloging-in-Publication Data
Didion, Joan.
[Essays, Selections]
Vintage Didion / Joan Didion.
p. cm.
Contents: Girl of the golden West—Arrival in San Salvador—The Metropolitan Cathredral in San Salvador, 1982—Miami one—Miami two—Miami three—In the realm of the Fisher King—Sentimental journeys—Clinton agonistes—Fixed opinions.
ISBN 1-4000-3393-4
I. Title.

PS3554.I33A6 2004
814'.54—dc21   2003053754

Book design by JoAnn Metsch

www.vintagebooks.com

Printed in the United States of America
10 9 8 7 6 5 4 3 2 1

APR 3 0 2004

PS
3554
.I 33
A6
2004

CONTENTS

VINTAGE **DIDION**

GIRL OF THE GOLDEN WEST

The domestic details spring to memory. Early on the evening of February 4, 1974, in her duplex apartment at 2603 Benvenue in Berkeley, Patricia Campbell Hearst, age nineteen, a student of art history at the University of California at Berkeley and a granddaughter of the late William Randolph Hearst, put on a blue terry-cloth bathrobe, heated a can of chicken-noodle soup and made tuna fish sandwiches for herself and her fiancé, Steven Weed; watched *Mission Impossible* and *The Magician* on television; cleaned up the dishes; sat down to study just as the doorbell rang; was abducted at gunpoint and held blindfolded, by three men and five women who called themselves the Symbionese Liberation Army, for the next fifty-seven days.

From the fifty-eighth day, on which she agreed to join her captors and was photographed in front of the SLA's cobra flag carrying a sawed-off M-1 carbine, until September 18, 1975, when she was arrested in San Francisco, Patricia Campbell Hearst participated actively in the rob-

beries of the Hibernia Bank in San Francisco and the
Crocker National Bank outside Sacramento; sprayed Cren-
shaw Boulevard in Los Angeles with a submachine gun to
cover a comrade apprehended for shoplifting; and was party
or witness to a number of less publicized thefts and several bombings, to which she would later refer as "actions,"
or "operations."

On trial in San Francisco for the Hibernia Bank operation she appeared in court wearing frosted-white nail
polish, and demonstrated for the jury the bolt action necessary to chamber an M-1. On a psychiatric test adminis-
tered while she was in custody she completed the
sentence "Most men . . ." with the words ". . . are ass-
holes." Seven years later she was living with the body-
guard she had married, their infant daughter, and two
German shepherds "behind locked doors in a Spanish-
style house equipped with the best electronic security system available," describing herself as "older and wiser,"
and dedicating her account of these events, *Every Secret
Thing,* to "Mom and Dad."

It was a special kind of sentimental education, a public
coming-of-age with an insistently literary cast to it, and it
seemed at the time to offer a parable for the period. Certain of its images entered the national memory. We had
Patricia Campbell Hearst in her first-communion dress,
smiling, and we had Patricia Campbell Hearst in the
Hibernia Bank surveillance stills, not smiling. We again
had her smiling in the engagement picture, an unremarkably pretty girl in a simple dress on a sunny lawn, and we

again had her not smiling in the "Tania" snapshot, the famous Polaroid with the M-1. We had her with her father and her sister Anne in a photograph taken at the Burlingame Country Club some months before the kidnapping: all three Hearsts smiling there, not only smiling but wearing leis, the father in maile and orchid leis, the daughters in pikake, that rarest and most expensive kind of lei, strand after strand of tiny Arabian jasmine buds strung like ivory beads.

We had the bank of microphones in front of the Hillsborough house whenever Randolph and Catherine Hearst ("Dad" and "Mom" in the first spectral messages from the absent daughter, "pig Hearsts" as the spring progressed) met the press, the potted flowers on the steps changing with the seasons, domestic upkeep intact in the face of crisis: azaleas, fuchsias, then cymbidium orchids massed for Easter. We had, early on, the ugly images of looting and smashed cameras and frozen turkey legs hurled through windows in West Oakland, the violent result of the Hearsts' first attempt to meet the SLA ransom demand, and we had, on television the same night, the news that William Knowland, the former United States senator from California and the most prominent member of the family that had run Oakland for half a century, had taken the pistol he was said to carry as protection against terrorists, positioned himself on a bank of the Russian River, and blown off the top of his head.

All of these pictures told a story, taught a dramatic lesson, carrying as they did the *frisson* of one another, the invitation to compare and contrast. The image of Patricia Campbell Hearst on the FBI "wanted" fliers was for example cropped from the image of the unremarkably pretty girl in the simple dress on the sunny lawn, schematic evidence that even a golden girl could be pinned in the beam of history. There was no actual connection between turkey legs thrown through windows in West Oakland and William Knowland lying facedown in the Russian River, but the paradigm was manifest, one California busy being born and another busy dying. Those cymbidiums on the Hearsts' doorstep in Hillsborough dissolved before our eyes into the image of a flaming palm tree in south-central Los Angeles (the model again was two Californias), the palm tree above the stucco bungalow in which Patricia Campbell Hearst was believed for a time to be burning to death on live television. (Actually, Patricia Campbell Hearst was in yet a third California, a motel room at Disneyland, watching the palm tree burn as we all were, on television, and it was Donald DeFreeze, Nancy Ling Perry, Angela Atwood, Patricia Soltysik, Camilla Hall, and William Wolfe, one black escaped convict and five children of the white middle class, who were dying in the stucco bungalow.)

Not only the images but the voice told a story, the voice on the tapes, the depressed voice with the California inflection, the voice that trailed off, now almost inaudible, then a hint of whine, a schoolgirl's sarcasm, a voice every parent recognized: *Mom, Dad. I'm OK. I had a few scrapes and stuff, but they washed them up. . . . I just hope you'll do what they say, Dad. . . . If you can get the food thing organized before the nineteenth then that's OK. . . . Whatever you come up with is basically OK, it was never intended that you feed the whole state. . . . I am here because I am a member of a ruling-class family and I think you can begin to see the analogy. . . . People should stop acting like I'm dead, Mom should get out of her black dress, that doesn't help at all. . . . Mom, Dad . . . I don't believe you're doing all you can . . . Mom, Dad . . . I'm starting to think that no one is concerned about me anymore. . . .* And then: *Greetings to the people. This is Tania.*

Patricia Campbell Hearst's great-grandfather had arrived in California by foot in 1850, unschooled, unmarried, thirty years old with few graces and no prospects, a Missouri farmer's son who would spend his thirties scratching around El Dorado and Nevada and Sacramento counties looking for a stake. In 1859 he found one, and at his death in 1891 George Hearst could leave the schoolteacher he had married in 1862 a fortune taken from the ground, the continuing proceeds from the most productive mines of the period, the Ophir in Nevada, the Homestake in South Dakota, the Ontario in Utah, the Anaconda in Montana, the San Luis in Mexico. The widow, Phoebe Apperson Hearst, a tiny, strong-minded woman then only forty-eight years old, took this apparently artesian income and financed her only child in the publishing empire he wanted, underwrote a surprising amount of the campus where her great-granddaughter would be enrolled at the time she was kidnapped, and built for herself, on sixty-seven thousand acres on the McCloud River in Siskiyou County, the original Wyntoon, a quarried-lava castle of which its architect, Bernard Maybeck, said simply: "Here you can reach all that is within you."

The extent to which certain places dominate the California imagination is apprehended, even by Californians, only dimly. Deriving not only from the landscape but from the claiming of it, from the romance of emigration, the radical abandonment of established attachments, this imagination remains obdurately symbolic, tending to locate lessons in what the rest of the country perceives only as scenery. Yosemite, for example, remains what Kevin Starr has called "one of the primary California symbols, a fixed factor of identity for all those who sought a primarily Californian aesthetic." Both the community of and the coastline at Carmel have a symbolic meaning lost to the contemporary visitor, a lingering allusion to art as freedom, freedom as craft, the "bohemian" pantheism of the early twentieth century. The Golden Gate Bridge, referring as it does to both the infinite and technology, suggests, to the Californian, a quite complex representation of land's end, and also of its beginning.

Patricia Campbell Hearst told us in *Every Secret Thing* that the place the Hearsts called Wyntoon was "a mystical land," "fantastic, otherworldly," "even more than San Simeon," which was in turn "so emotionally moving that it is still beyond my powers of description." That first Maybeck castle on the McCloud River was seen by most Californians only in photographs, and yet, before it burned in 1933, to be replaced by a compound of rather more playful Julia Morgan chalets ("Cinderella House," "Angel House," "Brown Bear House"), Phoebe Hearst's gothic Wyntoon and her son's baroque San Simeon seemed between them to embody certain opposing impulses in the local consciousness: northern and southern, wilderness sanctified and wilderness banished, the aggrandizement of nature and the aggrandizement of self. Wyntoon had mists, and allusions to the infinite, great trunks of trees left to rot where they fell, a wild river, barbaric fireplaces. San Simeon, swimming in sunlight and the here and now, had two swimming pools, and a zoo.

It was a family in which the romantic impulse would seem to have dimmed. Patricia Campbell Hearst told us that she "grew up in an atmosphere of clear blue skies, bright sunshine, rambling open spaces, long green lawns, large comfortable houses, country clubs with swimming pools and tennis courts and riding horses." At the Convent of the Sacred Heart in Menlo Park she told a nun to "go to hell," and thought herself "quite courageous, although very stupid." At Santa Catalina in Monterey she and Patricia Tobin, whose family founded one of the banks the SLA would later rob, skipped Benediction, and received "a load of demerits." Her father taught her to shoot, duck hunting. Her mother did not allow her to wear jeans into San Francisco. These were inheritors who tended to keep their names out of the paper, to exhibit not much interest in the world at large ("Who the hell is this guy again?" Randolph Hearst asked Steven Weed when the latter suggested trying to approach the SLA through Regis Debray, and then, when told, said, "We need a goddamn South American revolutionary mixed up in this thing like a hole in the head"), and to regard most forms of distinction with the reflexive distrust of the country club.

Yet if the Hearsts were no longer a particularly arresting California family, they remained embedded in the symbolic content of the place, and for a Hearst to be kidnapped from Berkeley, the very citadel of Phoebe Hearst's aspiration, was California as opera. "My thoughts at this time were focused on the single issue of survival," the heiress to Wyntoon and San Simeon told us about the fifty-seven days she spent in the closet. "Concerns over love and marriage, family life, friends, human relationships, my whole previous life, had really become, in SLA terms, bourgeois luxuries."

This abrupt sloughing of the past has, to the California ear, a distant echo, and the echo is of emigrant diaries. "Don't let this letter dishearten anybody, never take no cutoffs and hurry along as fast as you can," one of the surviving children of the Donner Party concluded her account of that crossing. "Don't worry about it," the author of *Every Secret Thing* reported having told herself in the closet after her first sexual encounter with a member of the SLA. "Don't examine your feelings. Never examine your feelings—they're no help at all." At the time Patricia Campbell Hearst was on trial in San Francisco, a number of psychiatrists were brought in to try to plumb what seemed to some an unsoundable depth in the narrative, that moment at which the victim binds over her fate to her captors. "She experienced what I call the death anxiety and the breaking point," Robert Jay Lifton, who was one of these psychiatrists, said. "Her external points of reference for maintenance of her personality had disappeared," Louis Jolyon West, another of the psychiatrists, said. Those were two ways of looking at it, and another was that Patricia Campbell Hearst had cut her losses and headed west, as her great-grandfather had before her.

The story she told in 1982 in *Every Secret Thing* was received, in the main, querulously, just as it had been when she told it during *The United States of America v. Patricia Campbell Hearst,* the 1976 proceeding during which she was tried for and convicted of the armed robbery of the Hibernia Bank (one count), and (the second count) the use of a weapon during the commission of a felony. Laconic, slightly ironic, resistant not only to the prosecution but to her own defense, Patricia Hearst was not, on trial in San Francisco, a conventionally ingratiating personality. "I don't know," I recall her saying over and over again during the few days I attended the trial. "I don't remember." "I suppose so." Had there not been, the prosecutor asked one day, telephones in the motels in which she had stayed when she drove across the country with Jack Scott? I recall Patricia Hearst looking at him as if she thought him deranged. I recall Randolph Hearst looking at the floor. I recall Catherine Hearst arranging a Galanos jacket over the back of her seat.

"Yes, I'm sure," their daughter said.

Where, the prosecutor asked, were these motels?

"One was . . . I think . . . " Patricia Hearst paused, and then: "Cheyenne? Wyoming?" She pronounced the names as if they were foreign, exotic, information registered and jettisoned. One of these motels had been in

Nevada, the place from which the Hearst money origi-
nally came: the heiress pronounced the name *Nevahda,*
like a foreigner.

In *Every Secret Thing* as at her trial, she seemed to project
an emotional distance, a peculiar combination of passiv-
ity and pragmatic recklessness ("I had crossed over. And I
would have to make the best of it . . . to live from day to
day, to do whatever they said, to play my part, and to pray
that I would survive") that many people found inexplicable and irritating. In 1982 as in 1976, she spoke only
abstractly about *why,* but quite specifically about *how.* "I
could not believe that I had actually fired that submachine
gun," she said of the incident in which she shot up Cren-
shaw Boulevard, but here was how she did it: "I kept
my finger pressed on the trigger until the entire clip of
thirty shots had been fired. . . . I then reached for my
own weapon, the semiautomatic carbine. I got off three
more shots. . . . "

And, after her book as after her trial, the questions
raised were not exactly about her veracity but about her
authenticity, her general intention, about whether she
was, as the assistant prosecutor put it during the trial, "for
real." This was necessarily a vain line of inquiry (whether
or not she "loved" William Wolfe was the actual point on
which the trial came to turn), and one that encouraged a
curious rhetorical regression among the inquisitors. "Why
did she choose to write this book?" Mark Starr asked
about *Every Secret Thing* in *Newsweek,* and then answered
himself: "Possibly she has inherited her family's journalistic sense of what will sell." "The rich get richer," Jane
Alpert concluded in *New York* magazine. "Patty," Ted

Morgan observed in the *New York Times Book Review,* "is now, thanks to the proceeds of her book, reverting to a more traditional family pursuit, capital formation."

These were dreamy notions of what a Hearst might do to turn a dollar, but they reflected a larger dissatisfaction, a conviction that the Hearst in question was telling less than the whole story, "leaving something out," although what the something might have been, given the doggedly detailed account offered in *Every Secret Thing,* would be hard to define. If "questions still linger," as they did for *Newsweek,* those questions were not about how to lace a bullet with cyanide: the way the SLA did it was to drill into the lead tip to a point just short of the gunpower, dip the tiny hole in a mound of cyanide crystals, and seal it with paraffin. If *Every Secret Thing* "creates more puzzles than it solves," as it did for Jane Alpert, those questions were not about how to make a pipe bomb: the trick here was to pack enough gunpowder into the pipe for a big bang and still leave sufficient oxygen for ignition, a problem, as Patricia Hearst saw it, of "devising the proper proportions of gunpowder, length of pipe and toaster wire, minus Teko's precious toilet paper." "Teko," or Bill Harris, insisted on packing his bombs with toilet paper, and, when one of them failed to explode under a police car in the Mission District, reacted with "one of his worst temper tantrums." Many reporters later found Bill and Emily Harris the appealing defendants that Patricia Hearst never was, but *Every Secret Thing* presented a convincing case for their being, as the author put it, not only "unattractive" but, her most pejorative adjective, "incompetent."

As notes from the underground go, Patricia Hearst's were eccentric in detail. She told us that Bill Harris's favorite television program was *S.W.A.T.* (one could, he said, "learn a lot about the pigs' tactics by watching these programs"); that Donald DeFreeze or "Cinque," drank plum wine from half-gallon jugs and listened to the radio for allusions to the revolution in song lyrics; and that Nancy Ling Perry, who was usually cast by the press in the rather glamorous role of "former cheerleader and Goldwater Girl," was four feet eleven inches tall, and affected a black accent. Emily Harris trained herself to "live with deprivation" by chewing only half sticks of gum. Bill Harris bought a yarmulke, under the impression that this was the way, during the sojourn in the Catskills after the Los Angeles shoot-out, to visit Grossinger's unnoticed.

Life with these people had the distorted logic of dreams, and Patricia Hearst seems to have accepted it with the wary acquiescence of the dreamer. Any face could turn against her. Any move could prove lethal. "My sisters and I had been brought up to believe that we were responsible for what we did and could not blame our transgressions on something being wrong inside our heads. I had joined the SLA because if I didn't they would have killed me. And I remained with them because I truly believed that the FBI would kill me if they could, and if not, the SLA would." She had, as she put it, crossed over. She would, as she put it, make the best of it, and not "reach back to family or friends."

This was the point on which most people foundered,

doubted her, found her least explicable, and it was also the point at which she was most specifically the child of a certain culture. Here is the single personal note in an emigrant diary kept by a relative of mine, William Kilgore, the journal of an overland crossing to Sacramento in 1850: "This is one of the trying mornings for me, as I now have to leave my family, or back out. Suffice it to say, we started." Suffice it to say. Don't examine your feelings, they're no help at all. Never take no cutoffs and hurry along as fast as you can. We need a goddamn South American revolutionary mixed up in this thing like a hole in the head. This was a California girl, and she was raised on a history that placed not much emphasis on *why*.

She was never an idealist, and this pleased no one. She was tainted by survival. She came back from the other side with a story no one wanted to hear, a dispiriting account of a situation in which delusion and incompetence were pitted against delusion and incompetence of another kind, and in the febrile rhythms of San Francisco in the mid-seventies it seemed a story devoid of high notes. The week her trial ended in 1976, the *San Francisco Bay Guardian* published an interview in which members of a collective called New Dawn expressed regret at her defection. "It's a question of your self-respect or your ass," one of them said. "If you choose your ass, you live with nothing." This idea that the SLA represented an idea worth defending (if only on the grounds that any idea must be better than none) was common enough at the time, although most people granted that the idea had gone awry. By March of

1977 another writer in the *Bay Guardian* was making a distinction between the "unbridled adventurism" of the SLA and the "discipline and skill" of the New World Liberation Front, whose "fifty-odd bombings without a casualty" made them a "definitely preferable alternative" to the SLA.

As it happened I had kept this issue of the *Bay Guardian,* dated March 31, 1977 (the *Bay Guardian* was not at the time a notably radical paper, by the way, but one that provided a fair guide to local tofu cookery and the mood of the community), and when I got it out to look at the piece on the SLA I noticed for the first time another piece: a long and favorable report on a San Francisco minister whose practice it was to "confront people and challenge their basic assumptions . . . as if he can't let the evil of the world pass him by, a characteristic he shares with other moral leaders." The minister, who was compared at one point to Cesar Chavez, was responsible, according to the writer, for a "mind-boggling" range of social service programs—food distribution, legal aid, drug rehabilitation, nursing homes, free Pap smears—as well as for a "twenty-seven-thousand-acre agricultural station." The agricultural station was in Guyana, and the minister of course was the Reverend Jim Jones, who eventually chose self-respect over his own and nine hundred other asses. This was another local opera, and one never spoiled by a protagonist who insisted on telling it her way.

—1982

ARRIVAL IN SAN SALVADOR, 1982

The three-year-old El Salvador International Airport is glassy and white and splendidly isolated, conceived during the waning of the Molina "National Transformation" as convenient less to the capital (San Salvador is forty miles away, until recently a drive of several hours) than to a central hallucination of the Molina and Romero regimes, the projected beach resorts, the Hyatt, the Pacific Paradise, tennis, golf, water-skiing, condos, *Costa del Sol;* the visionary invention of a tourist industry in yet another republic where the leading natural cause of death is gastrointestinal infection. In the general absence of tourists these hotels have since been abandoned, ghost resorts on the empty Pacific beaches, and to land at this airport built to service them is to plunge directly into a state in which no ground is solid, no depth of field reliable, no perception so definite that it might not dissolve into its reverse.

The only logic is that of acquiescence. Immigration is negotiated in a thicket of automatic weapons, but by whose authority the weapons are brandished (Army or

National Guard or National Police or Customs Police or Treasury Police or one of a continuing proliferation of other shadowy and overlapping forces) is a blurred point. Eye contact is avoided. Documents are scrutinized upside down. Once clear of the airport, on the new highway that slices through green hills rendered phosphorescent by the cloud cover of the tropical rainy season, one sees mainly underfed cattle and mongrel dogs and armored vehicles, vans and trucks and Cherokee Chiefs fitted with reinforced steel and bulletproof Plexiglas an inch thick. Such vehicles are a fixed feature of local life, and are popularly associated with disappearance and death. There was the Cherokee Chief seen following the Dutch television crew killed in Chalatenango province in March of 1982. There was the red Toyota three-quarter-ton pickup sighted near the van driven by the four American Catholic workers on the night they were killed in 1980. There were, in the late spring and summer of 1982, the three Toyota panel trucks, one yellow, one blue, and one green, none bearing plates, reported present at each of the mass detentions (a "detention" is another fixed feature of local life, and often precedes a "disappearance") in the Amatepec district of San Salvador. These are the details—the models and colors of armored vehicles, the makes and calibers of weapons, the particular methods of dismemberment and decapitation used in particular instances—on which the visitor to Salvador learns immediately to concentrate, to the exclusion of past or future concerns, as in a prolonged amnesiac fugue.

Terror is the given of the place. Black-and-white police cars cruise in pairs, each with the barrel of a rifle extruding from an open window. Roadblocks materialize at random, soldiers fanning out from trucks and taking positions, fingers always on triggers, safeties clicking on and off. Aim is taken as if to pass the time. Every morning *El Diario de Hoy* and *La Prensa Gráfica* carry cautionary stories. *"Una madre y sus dos hijos fueron asesinados con arma cortante (corvo) por ocho sujetos desconocidos el lunes en la noche"*: A mother and her two sons hacked to death in their beds by eight *desconocidos,* unknown men. The same morning's paper: the unidentified body of a young man, strangled, found on the shoulder of a road. Same morning, different story: the unidentified bodies of three young men, found on another road, their faces partially destroyed by bayonets, one face carved to represent a cross.

It is largely from these reports in the newspapers that the United States embassy compiles its body counts, which are transmitted to Washington in a weekly dispatch referred to by embassy people as "the grim-gram." These counts are presented in a kind of tortured code that fails to obscure what is taken for granted in El Salvador, that government forces do most of the killing. In a January 15, 1982 memo to Washington, for example, the embassy issued a "guarded" breakdown on its count of 6,909 "reported" political murders between September 16, 1980 and September 15, 1981. Of these 6,909, according to the memo, 922 were "believed committed by security forces," 952 "believed committed by leftist terrorists," 136 "believed committed by rightist terrorists," and 4,889 "committed by unknown assailants," the famous *desconocidos* favored by those San Salvador newspapers still publishing. (The figures actually add up not to 6,909 but to 6,899, leaving ten in a kind of official limbo.) The memo continued:

> "The uncertainty involved here can be seen in the fact that responsibility cannot be fixed in the majority of cases. We note, however, that it is generally believed in El Salvador that a large number of the unexplained killings are carried out by the security forces, officially or unofficially. The Embassy is aware of dramatic claims that have been made by one interest group or another in which the security forces figure as the primary agents of murder here. El Salvador's tangled web of attack and vengeance, traditional criminal violence and political mayhem make this an impossible charge to sustain. In saying this, however, we make no attempt to lighten the responsibility for the deaths of many hundreds, and perhaps thousands, which can be attributed to the security forces. . . ."

The body count kept by what is generally referred to in San Salvador as "the Human Rights Commission" is higher than the embassy's, and documented periodically by a photographer who goes out looking for bodies. These bodies he photographs are often broken into unnatural positions, and the faces to which the bodies are attached (when they are attached) are equally unnatural, sometimes unrecognizable as human faces, obliterated by acid or beaten to a mash of misplaced ears and teeth or slashed ear to ear and invaded by insects. *Encontrado en Antiguo Cuscatlán el día 25 de Marzo 1982; camison de dormir celeste,"* the typed caption reads on one photograph: found in Antiguo Cuscatlán March 25, 1982 wearing a sky-blue nightshirt. The captions are laconic. Found in Soyapango May 21, 1982. Found in Mejicanos June 11, 1982. Found at El Playón May 30, 1982, white shirt, purple pants, black shoes.

The photograph accompanying that last caption shows a body with no eyes, because the vultures got to it before the photographer did. There is a special kind of practical information that the visitor to El Salvador acquires immediately, the way visitors to other places acquire information about the currency rates, the hours for the museums. In El Salvador one learns that vultures go first for the soft tissue, for the eyes, the exposed genitalia, the open mouth. One learns that an open mouth can be used to make a specific point, can be stuffed with something emblematic; stuffed, say, with a penis, or, if the point has to do with land title, stuffed with some of the dirt in question. One learns that hair deteriorates less rapidly than flesh, and that a skull surrounded by a perfect corona of hair is a not uncommon sight in the body dumps.

All forensic photographs induce in the viewer a certain protective numbness, but dissociation is more difficult here. In the first place these are not, technically, "forensic" photographs, since the evidence they document will never be presented in a court of law. In the second place the disfigurement is too routine. The locations are too near, the dates too recent. There is the presence of the relatives of the disappeared: the women who sit every day in this cramped office on the grounds of the archdiocese, waiting to look at the spiral-bound photo albums in which the photographs are kept. These albums have plastic covers bearing soft-focus color photographs of young Americans in dating situations (strolling through autumn foliage on one album, recumbent in a field of daisies on another), and the women, looking for the bodies of their husbands and brothers and sisters and children, pass them from hand to hand without comment or expression.

"One of the more shadowy elements of the violent scene here [is] the death squad. Existence of these groups has long been disputed, but not by many Salvadorans. . . . Who constitutes the death squads is yet another difficult question. We do not believe that these squads exist as permanent formations but rather as ad hoc vigilante groups that coalesce according to perceived need. Membership is also uncertain, but in addition to civilians we believe that both on- and off-duty members of the security forces are participants. This was unofficially confirmed by right-wing spokesman Maj. Roberto D'Aubuisson who stated in an interview in early 1981 that security force members utilize the guise of the death squad when a potentially embarrassing or odious task needs to be performed."

—*From the confidential but later declassified January 15, 1982 memo previously cited, drafted for the State Department by the political section at the embassy in San Salvador.*

The dead and pieces of the dead turn up in El Salvador everywhere, every day, as taken for granted as in a nightmare, or a horror movie. Vultures of course suggest the presence of a body. A knot of children on the street suggests the presence of a body. Bodies turn up in the brush of vacant lots, in the garbage thrown down ravines in the richest districts, in public rest rooms, in bus stations. Some are dropped in Lake Ilopango, a few miles east of the city, and wash up near the lakeside cottages and clubs frequented by what remains in San Salvador of the sporting bourgeoisie. Some still turn up at El Playón, the lunar lava field of rotting human flesh visible at one time or another on every television screen in America but characterized in June of 1982 in the *El Salvador News Gazette,* an English-language weekly edited by an American named Mario Rosenthal, as an "uncorroborated story . . . dredged up from the files of leftist propaganda." Others turn up at Puerta del Diablo, above Parque Balboa, a national *Turicentro* described as recently as the April–July 1982 issue of *Aboard TACA,* the magazine provided passengers on the national airline of El Salvador, as "offering excellent subjects for color photography."

I drove up to Puerta del Diablo one morning in June of 1982, past the Casa Presidencial and the camouflaged watchtowers and heavy concentrations of troops and arms south of town, on up a narrow road narrowed further by landslides and deep crevices in the roadbed, a drive so insistently premonitory that after a while I began to hope that I would pass Puerta del Diablo without knowing it, just miss it, write it off, turn around and go back. There was, however, no way of missing it. Puerta del Diablo is a "view site" in an older and distinctly literary tradition, nature as lesson, an immense cleft rock through which half of El Salvador seems framed, a site so romantic and "mystical," so theatrically sacrificial in aspect, that

it might be a cosmic parody of nineteenth-century landscape painting. The place presents itself as pathetic fallacy:
the sky "broods," the stones "weep," a constant seepage of
water weighting the ferns and moss. The foliage is thick
and slick with moisture. The only sound is a steady buzz,
I believe of cicadas.

Body dumps are seen in El Salvador as a kind of visitors' must-do, difficult but worth the detour. "Of course
you have seen El Playón," an aide to President Alvaro
Magaña said to me one day, and proceeded to discuss the
site geologically, as evidence of the country's geothermal resources. He made no mention of the bodies. I was
unsure if he was sounding me out or simply found the
geothermal aspect of overriding interest. One difference
between El Playón and Puerta del Diablo is that most
bodies at El Playón appear to have been killed somewhere
else, and then dumped; at Puerta del Diablo the execu-
tions are believed to occur in place, at the top, and the
bodies thrown over. Sometimes reporters will speak of
wanting to spend the night at Puerta del Diablo, in order
to document the actual execution, but at the time I was
in Salvador no one had.

The aftermath, the daylight aspect, is well documented.
"Nothing fresh today, I hear," an embassy officer said
when I mentioned that I had visited Puerta del Diablo.
"Were there any on top?" someone else asked. "There
were supposed to have been three on top yesterday." The
point about whether or not there had been any on top
was that usually it was necessary to go down to see bodies. The way down is hard. Slabs of stone, slippery with
moss, are set into the vertiginous cliff, and it is down this

cliff that one begins the descent to the bodies, or what is left of the bodies, pecked and maggoty masses of flesh, bone, hair. On some days there have been helicopters circling, tracking those making the descent. Other days there have been militia at the top, in the clearing where the road seems to run out, but on the morning I was there the only people on top were a man and a woman and three small children, who played in the wet grass while the woman started and stopped a Toyota pickup. She appeared to be learning how to drive. She drove forward and then back toward the edge, apparently following the man's signals, over and over again.

We did not speak, and it was only later, down the mountain and back in the land of the provisionally living, that it occurred to me that there was a definite question about why a man and a woman might choose a well-known body dump for a driving lesson. This was one of a number of occasions, during the two weeks my husband and I spent in El Salvador, on which I came to understand, in a way I had not understood before, the exact mechanism of terror.

—1983

During the week before I flew down to El Salvador a Salvadoran woman who works for my husband and me in Los Angeles gave me repeated instructions about what we must and must not do. We must not go out at night. We must stay off the street whenever possible. We must never ride in buses or taxis, never leave the capital, never imagine that our passports would protect us. We must not even consider the hotel a safe place: people were killed in hotels. She spoke with considerable vehemence, because two of her brothers had been killed in Salvador in August of 1981, in their beds. The throats of both brothers had been slashed. Her father had been cut but stayed alive. Her mother had been beaten. Twelve of her other relatives, aunts and uncles and cousins, had been taken from their houses one night the same August, and their bodies had been found some time later, in a ditch. I assured her that we would remember, we would be careful, we would in fact be so careful that we would probably (trying for a light touch) spend all our time in church.

She became still more agitated, and I realized that I had spoken as a *norteamericana:* churches had not been to this woman the neutral ground they had been to me. I must remember: Archbishop Romero killed saying mass in the chapel of the Divine Providence Hospital in San Salvador. I must remember: more than thirty people killed at Archbishop Romero's funeral in the Metropolitan Cathedral in San Salvador. I must remember: more than twenty people killed before that on the steps of the Metropolitan Cathedral. CBS had filmed it. It had been on television, the bodies jerking, those still alive crawling over the dead as they tried to get out of range. I must understand: the Church was dangerous.

I told her that I understood, that I knew all that, and I did, abstractly, but the specific meaning of the Church she knew eluded me until I was actually there, at the Metropolitan Cathedral in San Salvador, one afternoon when rain sluiced down its corrugated plastic windows and puddled around the supports of the Sony and Phillips billboards near the steps. The effect of the Metropolitan Cathedral is immediate, and entirely literary. This is the cathedral that the late Archbishop Oscar Arnulfo Romero refused to finish, on the premise that the work of the Church took precedence over its display, and the high walls of raw concrete bristle with structural rods, rusting now, staining the concrete, sticking out at wrenched and violent angles. The wiring is exposed. Fluorescent tubes hang askew. The great high altar is backed by warped plyboard. The cross on the altar is of bare incandescent bulbs, but the bulbs, that afternoon, were unlit: there was in fact no light at all on the main altar, no light on the cross, no light on the globe of the world that showed the northern American continent in gray and the southern in white; no light on the dove above the globe, *Salvador del Mundo*. In this vast brutalist space that was the cathedral, the unlit altar seemed to offer a single ineluctable message: at this time and in this place the light of the world could be construed as out, off, extinguished.

In many ways the Metropolitan Cathedral is an authentic piece of political art, a statement for El Salvador as *Guernica* was for Spain. It is quite devoid of sentimental relief. There are no decorative or architectural references to familiar parables, in fact no stories at all, not even the Stations of the Cross. On the afternoon I was there the flowers laid on the altar were dead. There were no traces of normal parish activity. The doors were open to the barricaded main steps, and down the steps there was a spill of red paint, lest anyone forget the blood shed there. Here and there on the cheap linoleum inside the cathedral there was what seemed to be actual blood, dried in spots, the kind of spots dropped by a slow hemorrhage, or by a woman who does not know or does not care that she is menstruating.

There were several women in the cathedral during the hour or so I spent there, a young woman with a baby, an older woman in house slippers, a few others, all in black. One of the women walked the aisles as if by compulsion, up and down, across and back, crooning loudly as she walked. Another knelt without moving at the tomb of Archbishop Romero in the right transept. "Loor a Monsenor Romero," the crude needlepoint tapestry by the tomb read, "Praise to Monsignor Romero from the

Mothers of the Imprisoned, the Disappeared, and the Murdered," the *Comité de Madres y Familiares de Presos, Desaparecidos, y Asesinados Politicos de El Salvador.*

The tomb itself was covered with offerings and petitions, notes decorated with motifs cut from greeting cards and cartoons. I recall one with figures cut from a Bugs Bunny strip, and another with a pencil drawing of a baby in a crib. The baby in this drawing seemed to be receiving medication or fluid or blood intravenously, through the IV line shown in its wrist. I studied the notes for a while and then went back and looked again at the unlit altar, and at the red paint on the main steps, from which it was possible to see the guardsmen on the balcony of the National Palace hunching back to avoid the rain. Many Salvadorans are offended by the Metropolitan Cathedral, which is as it should be, because the place remains perhaps the only unambiguous political statement in El Salvador, a metaphorical bomb in the ultimate power station.

—1983

MIAMI ONE

Havana vanities come to dust in Miami. On the August night in 1933 when General Gerardo Machado, then president of Cuba, flew out of Havana into exile, he took with him five revolvers, seven bags of gold, and five friends, still in their pajamas. Gerardo Machado is buried now in a marble crypt at Woodlawn Park Cemetery in Miami, Section Fourteen, the mausoleum. On the March night in 1952 when Carlos Prío Socarrás, who had helped depose Gerardo Machado in 1933 and had fifteen years later become president himself, flew out of Havana into exile, he took with him his foreign minister, his minister of the interior, his wife and his two small daughters. A photograph of the occasion shows Señora de Prío, quite beautiful, boarding the plane in what appears to be a raw silk suit, and a hat with black fishnet veiling. She wears gloves, and earrings. Her makeup is fresh. The husband and father, recently the president, wears dark glasses, and carries the younger child, María Elena, in his arms.

Carlos Prío is now buried himself at Woodlawn Park

Cemetery in Miami, Section Three, not far from Gerardo Machado, in a grave marked by a six-foot marble stone on which the flag of Cuba waves in red, white, and blue ceramic tile. CARLOS PRÍO SOCARRÁS 1903–1977, the stone reads, and directly below that, as if Carlos Prío Socarrás's main hedge against oblivion had been that period at the University of Havana when he was running actions against Gerardo Machado: MIEMBRO DEL DIRECTORIO ESTUDIANTIL UNIVERSITARIO 1930. Only then does the legend PRESIDENTE DE LA REPÚBLICA DE CUBA 1948–1952 appear, an anticlimax. Presidencies are short and the glamours of action long, there among the fallen frangipani and crepe myrtle blossoms at Woodlawn Park Cemetery in Miami. "They say that I was a terrible president of Cuba," Carlos Prío once said to Arthur M. Schlesinger, Jr., during a visit to the Kennedy White House some ten years into the quarter-century Miami epilogue to his four-year Havana presidency. "That may be true. But I was the best president Cuba ever had."

Many Havana epilogues have been played in Florida, and some prologues. Florida is that part of the Cuban stage where declamatory exits are made, and side deals. Florida is where the chorus waits to comment on the action, and sometimes to join it. The exiled José Martí raised money among the Cuban tobacco workers in Key West and Tampa, and in 1894 attempted to mount an invasionary expedition from north of Jacksonville. The exiled Fidel Castro Ruz came to Miami in 1955 for money to take the 26 Julio into the Sierra Maestra, and got it, from Carlos

Prío. Fulgencio Batista had himself come back from Florida to take Havana away from Carlos Prío in 1952, but by 1958 Fidel Castro, with Carlos Prío's money, was taking it away from Fulgencio Batista, at which turn Carlos Prío's former prime minister tried to land a third force in Camagüey Province, the idea being to seize the moment from Fidel Castro, a notably failed undertaking encouraged by the Central Intelligence Agency and financed by Carlos Prío, at home in Miami Beach.

This is all instructive. In the continuing opera still called, even by Cubans who have now lived the largest part of their lives in this country, *el exilio,* the exile, meetings at private houses in Miami Beach are seen to have consequences. The actions of individuals are seen to affect events directly. Revolutions and counterrevolutions are framed in the private sector, and the state security apparatus exists exclusively to be enlisted by one or another private player. That this particular political style, indigenous to the Caribbean and to Central America, has now been naturalized in the United States is one reason why, on the flat coastal swamps of South Florida, where the palmettos once blew over the detritus of a dozen failed booms and the hotels were boarded up six months a year, there has evolved since the early New Year's morning in 1959 when Fulgencio Batista flew for the last time out of Havana (for this flight, to the Dominican Republic on an Aerovías Q DC-4, the women still wore the evening dresses in which they had gone to dinner) a settlement of considerable interest, not exactly an American city as American cities have until recently been understood but a tropical capital: long on rumor, short on memory, overbuilt on the chimera of runaway money and referring not to New York or Boston or Los Angeles or Atlanta but to Caracas and Mexico, to Havana and to Bogotá and to Paris and Madrid. Of American cities Miami has since 1959 connected only to Washington, which is the peculiarity of both places, and increasingly the warp.

—1987

MIAMI TWO

Guillermo Novo was known to FBI agents and federal prosecutors and the various personnel who made up "terrorist task forces" on the eastern seaboard of the United States as one of the Novo brothers, Ignacio and Guillermo, two exiles who first came to national attention in 1964, when they fired a dud bazooka shell at the United Nations during a speech by Che Guevara. There were certain farcical elements here (the embattled brothers bobbing in a small boat, the shell plopping harmlessly into the East River), and, in a period when Hispanics were seen by many Americans as intrinsically funny, an accent joke, this incident was generally treated tolerantly, a comic footnote to the news. As time went by, however, the names of the Novo brothers began turning up in less comic footnotes, for example this one, on page 93 of volume X of the report made by the House Select Committee on Assassinations on its 1978 investigation of the assassination of John F. Kennedy:

(67) Immunized executive session testimony of Marita Lorenz, May 31, 1978. Hearings before the House Select Committee on Assassinations. Lorenz, who had publicly claimed she was once Castro's mistress (*Miami News,* June 15, 1976), told the committee she was present at a September 1963 meeting in Orlando Bosch's Miami home during which Lee Harvey Oswald, Frank Sturgis, Pedro Diaz Lanz, and Bosch made plans to go to Dallas. . . . She further testified that around November 15, 1963, she, Jerry Patrick Hemming, the Novo brothers, Pedro Diaz Lanz, Sturgis, Bosch, and Oswald traveled in a two-car caravan to Dallas and stayed in a motel where they were contacted by Jack Ruby. There were several rifles and scopes in the motel room. . . . Lorenz said she returned to Miami around November 19 or 20. . . . The committee found no evidence to support Lorenz's allegation.

Guillermo Novo himself was among those convicted, in a 1979 trial that rested on the demonstration of connections between the Cuban defendants and DINA, the Chilean secret police, of the assassination in Washington of the former Chilean diplomat Orlando Letelier and of the Institute for Policy Studies researcher who happened to be with him when his car blew up, Ronni Moffitt. This conviction was overturned on appeal (the appellate court ruled that the testimony of two jailhouse informants had been improperly admitted), and in a 1981 retrial, after the federal prosecutors turned down a deal in which the defense offered a plea of guilty on the lesser charge of conspiracy, plus what Guillermo Novo's attorney called "a sweetener," a "guarantee" by Guillermo Novo "to stop all violence by Cuban exiles in the United States," Guillermo Novo was acquitted.

I happened to meet Guillermo Novo in 1985, one Monday morning when I was waiting for someone in the reception room at WRHC–Cadena Azul, Miami, a station the call letters of which stood for Radio Havana Cuba. There was about this meeting nothing of either moment or consequence. A man who introduced himself as "Bill Novo" just appeared beside me, and we exchanged minor biography for a few minutes. He said that he had noticed me reading a letter framed on the wall of the reception room. He said that he was the sales manager for WRHC, and had lived in Miami only three years. He said that he had, however, lived in the United States since 1954, mostly in New York and New Jersey. He was a small sharp-featured man in a white tropical suit, who in fact spoke English with an accent that suggested New Jersey, and he had a way of materializing and dematerializing sideways, of appearing from and then sidling back into an inner office, which was where he retreated after he gave me his business card, the exchange of cards remaining a more or less fixed ritual in Cuban Miami. GUILLERMO NOVO SAMPOL, the card read. *Gerente de Ventas, WRHC–Cadena Azul.*

That it was possible on a Monday morning in Miami to have so desultory an encounter with one of the Novo brothers seemed to me, perhaps because I was not yet accustomed to a rhythm in which dealings with DINA and unsupported allegations about Dallas motel rooms could be incorporated into the American business day, remarkable, and later that week I asked an exile acquaintance who was familiar with WRHC if the Guillermo Novo who was the sales manager there was in fact the Guillermo Novo who had been tried in the Letelier assassination. There had been, my acquaintance demurred, "a final acquittal on the Letelier count." But it was, I persisted, the same man. My acquaintance had shrugged impatiently, not as if he thought it best not mentioned, but as if he did not quite see the interest. "Bill Novo has been a man of action," he said. "Yes. Of course."

To be a man of action in Miami was to receive encouragement from many quarters. On the wall of the reception room at WRHC–Cadena Azul, Miami, where the sales manager was Guillermo Novo and an occasional commentator was Fidel and Raúl Castro's estranged sister Juanita and the host of the most popular talk show was Felipe Rivero, whose family had from 1832 until 1960 published the powerful *Diario de la Marina* in Havana and who would in 1986, after a controversy fueled by his insistence that the Holocaust had not occurred but had been fabricated "to defame and divide the German people," move from WRHC to WOCN, there hung in 1985 a framed letter, the letter Guillermo Novo had mentioned when he first materialized that Monday morning. This letter, which was dated October 1983 and signed by the president of the United States, read:

I learned from Becky Dunlop [presumably Becky Norton Dunlop, a White House aide who later followed

Edwin Meese to the Justice Department] about the outstanding work being done at WRHC. Many of your
listeners have also been in touch, praising your news
coverage and your editorials. Your talented staff deserves
special commendation for keeping your listeners well-
informed.

I've been particularly pleased, of course, that you have
been translating and airing a Spanish version of my weekly
talks. This is important because your signal reaches the
people of Cuba, whose rigidly controlled government
media suppress any news Castro and his communist
henchmen do not want them to know. WRHC is per-
forming a great service for all its listeners. Keep up the
good work, and God bless you.

[signed] RONALD REAGAN

At the time I first noticed it on the WRHC wall, and
attracted Guillermo Novo's attention by reading it, this
letter interested me because I had the week before been
looking back through the administration's arguments for
Radio Martí, none of which, built as they were on the
figure of beaming light into utter darkness, had alluded to
these weekly talks that the people of Cuba appeared to be
getting on WRHC–Cadena Azul, Miami. Later the letter
interested me because I had begun reading back through
the weekly radio talks themselves, and had come across
one from 1978 in which Ronald Reagan, not yet president, had expressed his doubt that either the Pinochet
government or the indicted "Cuban anti-Castro exiles,"

one of whom had been Guillermo Novo, had anything to do with the Letelier assassination.

Ronald Reagan had wondered instead ("I don't know the answer, but it is a question worth asking. . . .") if Orlando Letelier's "connections with Marxists and far-left causes" might not have set him up for assassination, caused him to be, as the script for this talk put it, "murdered by his own masters." Here was the scenario: "Alive," Ronald Reagan had reasoned in 1978, Orlando Letelier "could be compromised; dead he could become a martyr. And the left didn't lose a minute in making him one." Actually this version of the Letelier assassination had first been advanced by Senator Jesse Helms (R-N.C.), who had advised his colleagues on the Senate floor that it was not "plausible" to suspect the Pinochet government in the Letelier case, because terrorism was "most often an organized tool of the left," but the Reagan reworking was interesting on its own, a way of speaking, later to become familiar, in which events could be revised as they happened into illustrations of ideology.

"There was no blacklist of Hollywood," Ronald Reagan told Robert Scheer of the *Los Angeles Times* during the 1980 campaign. "The blacklist in Hollywood, if there was one, was provided by the communists." "I'm going to voice a suspicion now that I've never said aloud before," Ronald Reagan told thirty-six high-school students in Washington in 1983 about death squads in El Salvador. "I wonder if all of this is right wing, or if those guerrilla forces have not realized that by infiltrating into the city of San Salvador and places like that, they can get away with these violent acts, helping to try and bring down the government, and the right wing will be blamed for it." "New intelligence shows," Ronald Reagan told his Saturday radio listeners in March of 1986, by way of explaining why he was asking Congress to provide "the Nicaraguan freedom fighters" with what he called "the means to fight back," that "Tomás Borge, the communist interior minister, is engaging in a brutal campaign to bring the freedom fighters into discredit. You see, Borge's communist operatives dress in freedom fighter uniforms, go into the countryside and murder and mutilate ordinary Nicaraguans."

Such stories were what David Gergen, when he was the White House communications director, had once called "a folk art," the President's way of "trying to tell us how society works." Other members of the White House staff had characterized these stories as the President's "notions," casting them in the genial framework of random avuncular musings, but they were something more than that. In the first place they were never random, but systematic and rather energetically so. The stories were told to a single point. The language in which the stories were told was not that of political argument but of advertising ("New intelligence shows . . ." and "Now it has been learned . . ." and, a construction that got my attention in a 1984 address to the National Religious Broadcasters, "Medical science doctors confirm . . ."), of the sales pitch.

This was not just a vulgarity of diction. When someone speaks of Orlando Letelier as "murdered by his own masters," or of the WRHC signal reaching a people denied information by "Castro and his communist henchmen," or of the "freedom fighter uniforms" in which the "communist operatives" of the "communist interior minister" disguise themselves, that person is not arguing a case, but counting instead on the willingness of the listener to enter what Hannah Arendt called, in a discussion of propaganda, "the gruesome quiet of an entirely imaginary world." On the morning I met Guillermo Novo in the reception room at WRHC–Cadena Azul I copied the framed commendation from the White House into my notebook, and later typed it out and pinned it to my own office wall, an aide-mémoire to the distance between what is said in the high ether of Washington, which is about the making of those gestures and the sending of those messages and the drafting of those positions that will serve to maintain that imaginary world, about two-track strategies and alternative avenues and Special Groups (Augmented), about "not breaking faith" and "making it clear," and what is heard on the ground in Miami, which is about consequences.

In many ways Miami remains our most graphic lesson in consequences. "I can assure you that this flag will be returned to this brigade in a free Havana," John F. Kennedy said to the surviving members of the 2506 Brigade at the Orange Bowl in 1962 (the "supposed promise," the promise "not in the script," the promise "made in the emotion of the day"), meaning it as an abstraction, the rhetorical expression of a collective wish; a kind of poetry, which of course makes nothing happen. "We will not permit the Soviets and their henchmen in Havana to deprive others of their freedom," Ronald Reagan said at the Dade County Auditorium in 1983 (2,500 people inside, 60,000 outside, 12 standing ovations and a *pollo asado* lunch at La Esquina de Tejas with Jorge Mas Canosa and 203 other provisional loyalists), and then Ronald Reagan, the first American president since John F. Kennedy to visit Miami in search of Cuban support, added this: "Someday, Cuba itself will be free."

This was of course just more poetry, another rhetorical expression of the same collective wish, but Ronald Reagan, like John F. Kennedy before him, was speaking here to people whose historical experience has not been that poetry makes nothing happen. On one of the first evenings I spent in Miami I sat at midnight over *carne con papas* in an art-filled condominium in one of the Arquitectonica buildings on Brickell Avenue and listened to several exiles talk about the relationship of what was said in Washington to what was done in Miami. These exiles were all well-educated. They were well-read, well-traveled, comfortable citizens of a larger world than that of either Miami or Washington, with well-cut blazers and French dresses and interests in New York and Madrid and Mexico. Yet what was said that evening in the expensive condominium overlooking Biscayne Bay proceeded from an almost primitive helplessness, a regressive fury at having been, as these exiles saw it, repeatedly used and repeatedly betrayed by the government of the United States. "Let me tell you something," one of them said. "They talk about 'Cuban terrorists.' The guys they call 'Cuban terrorists' are the guys they trained."

This was not, then, the general exile complaint about a

government that might have taken up their struggle but had not. This was something more specific, a complaint that the government in question had in fact taken up *la lucha,* but for its own purposes, and, in what these exiles saw as a pattern of deceit stretching back through six administrations, to its own ends. The pattern, as they saw it, was one in which the government of the United States had repeatedly encouraged or supported exile action and then, when policy shifted and such action became an embarrassment, a discordant note in whatever message Washington was sending that month or that year, had discarded the exiles involved, had sometimes not only discarded them but, since the nature of *la lucha* was essentially illegal, turned them in, set them up for prosecution; positioned them, as it were, for the fall.

They mentioned, as many exiles did, the Omega 7 prosecutions. They mentioned, as many exiles did, the Cuban burglars at the Watergate, who were told, because so many exiles had come by that time to distrust the CIA, that the assignment at hand was not just CIA, but straight from the White House. They mentioned the case of Jose Elias de la Torriente, a respected exile leader who had been, in the late 1960s, recruited by the CIA to lend his name and his prestige to what was set forth as a new plan to overthrow Fidel Castro, the "Work Plan for Liberation," or the Torriente Plan.

Money had once again been raised, and expectations. The entire attention of *el exilio* had for a time been focused on the Torriente Plan, a diversion of energy that, as years passed and nothing happened, suggested to many that what the plan may have been from its inception was just another ad hoc solution to the disposal problem, another mirror trick. Jose Elias de la Torriente had been called, by a frustrated community once again left with nowhere to go, a traitor. Jose Elias de la Torriente had been called a CIA stooge. Jose Elias de la Torriente had finally been, at age seventy, as he sat in his house in Coral Gables watching *The Robe* on television about nine o'clock on the evening of Good Friday, 1974, assassinated, shot through the venetian blind on a window by someone, presumably an exile, who claimed the kill in the name "Zero."

This had, in the telling at the dinner table, the sense of a situation played out to its Aristotelian end, of that inexorable Caribbean progress from cause to effect that I later came to see as central to the way Miami thought about itself. Miami stories tended to have endings. The cannon onstage tended to be fired. One of those who spoke most ardently that evening was a quite beautiful young woman in a white jersey dress, a lawyer, active in Democratic politics in Miami. This dinner in the condominium overlooking Biscayne Bay took place in March of 1985, and the woman in the white jersey dress was María Elena Prío Durán, the child who flew into exile in March of 1952 with her father's foreign minister, her father's minister of the interior, her father, her sister, and her mother, the equally beautiful woman in the hat with the fishnet veiling.

I recall watching María Elena Prío Durán that night as she pushed back her hair and reached across the table for a cigarette. This was a long time before the C-123K carrying Eugene Hasenfus fell from the sky inside Nicaragua. This was a long time before Eugene Hasenfus mentioned the names of the 2506 members already in place at Ilopango. NICARAGUA HOY, CUBA MAÑANA. Let me tell you about Cuban terrorists, another of the exiles at dinner that night, a prominent Miami architect named Raúl Rodríguez, was saying at the end of the table. Cuba never grew plastique. Cuba grew tobacco. Cuba grew sugarcane. Cuba never grew C-4. María Elena Prío Durán lit the cigarette and immediately crushed it out. C-4, Raúl Rodríguez said, and he slammed his palm down on the white tablecloth as he said it, grew here.

—*1987*

MIAMI THREE

Steven Carr was, at twenty-six, a South Florida lowlife, a sometime Naples construction worker with the motto DEATH BEFORE DISHONOR and a flaming skull tattooed on his left biceps; a discharge from the Navy for alcohol abuse; and a grand-theft conviction for stealing two gold-and-diamond rings, valued at $578, given to his mother by his stepfather. "She only wore them on holidays, I thought she'd never notice they were gone," Steven Carr later said about the matter of his mother's rings. He did not speak Spanish. He had no interest in any side of the conflict in Nicaragua. Nonetheless, in March of 1985, according to the story he began telling after he had been arrested in Costa Rica on weapons charges and was awaiting trial at La Reforma prison in San José, Steven Carr had collected arms for the contras at various locations around Dade County, loaded them onto a chartered Convair 440 at Fort Lauderdale–Hollywood International Airport, accompanied this shipment to Ilopango airport in San Salvador, and witnessed the eventual delivery of the arms to a unit of 2506 veterans fighting with the contras from a base about three miles south of the Nicaraguan border.

This story later became familiar, but its significance at the time Steven Carr first told it, in the summer of 1985 to Juan Tamayo of the *Miami Herald,* was that he was the first person to publicly claim firsthand knowledge of all stages of a single shipment. By the summer of 1986, after Steven Carr had bonded out of La Reforma and was back in South Florida (the details of how he got there were disputed, but either did or did not involve American embassy officials in Panama and San José who either did or did not give him a plane ticket and instructions to "get the hell out of Dodge"), doing six months in the Collier County jail for violation of probation on the outstanding matter of his mother's rings, he was of course telling it as well to investigators from various congressional committees and from the U.S. attorney's office in Miami. This was the point, in August 1986, at which his lawyers asked that he be released early and placed, on the grounds that the story he was telling endangered his life, in a witness protection program. "I'm not too popular with a lot of people because I'm telling the truth," Steven Carr told the *Miami Herald* a few days before his petition was heard and denied. "I wouldn't feel very safe just walking the streets after all this is over."

Steven Carr was released from the Collier County jail, having served his full sentence, on November 20, 1986. Twenty-three days later, at two-thirty on the morning of December 13, 1986, Steven Carr collapsed outside the room he was renting in Panorama City, California (a room that, according to the woman from whom he had rented it, Jackie Scott, he rarely left, and in which he slept with the doors locked and the lights on), convulsed, and died, of an apparent cocaine overdose. "I'm sorry," Steven Carr had said when Jackie Scott, whose daughter had heard "a commotion" and woken her, found him lying in the driveway. Jackie Scott told the *Los Angeles Times* that she had not seen Steven Carr drinking or taking drugs that evening, nor could she shed any light on what he had said next: "I paranoided out—I ate it all."

Jesus Garcia was a former Dade County corrections officer who was, at the time he began telling his story early in 1986, doing time in Miami for illegal possession of a MAC-10 with silencer. Jesus Garcia, who had been born in the United States of Cuban parents and thought of himself as a patriot, talked about having collected arms for the contras during the spring of 1985, and also about the plan, which he said had been discussed in the cocktail lounge of the Howard Johnson's near the Miami airport in February of 1985, to assassinate the new American ambassador to Costa Rica, blow up the embassy there, and blame it on the Sandinistas. The idea, Jesus Garcia said, had been to give the United States the opportunity it needed to invade Nicaragua, and also to collect on a million-dollar contract the Colombian cocaine cartel was said to have out on the new American ambassador to Costa Rica, who had recently been the American ambassador to Colombia and had frequently spoken of what he called "narco-guerrillas."

There were in the story told by Jesus Garcia and in the story told by Steven Carr certain details that appeared to coincide. Both Jesus Garcia and Steven Carr mentioned the Howard Johnson's near the Miami airport, which happened also to be the Howard Johnson's with the seventeen-dollar-a-night "guerrilla discount." Both Jesus Garcia and Steven Carr mentioned meetings in Miami with an American named Bruce Jones, who was said to own a farm on the border between Costa Rica and Nicaragua. Both Jesus Garcia and Steven Carr mentioned Thomas Posey, the Alabama produce wholesaler who had founded the paramilitary group CMA, or Civilian Materiel Assistance, formerly Civilian Military Assistance. Both Jesus Garcia and Steven Carr mentioned Robert Owen, the young Stanford graduate who had gone to Washington to work on the staff of Senator Dan Quayle (R-Ind.), had then moved into public relations, at Gray and Company, had in January of 1985 founded the nonprofit Institute for Democracy, Education, and Assistance, or IDEA (which was by the fall of 1985 on a consultancy contract to the State Department's Nicaraguan Humanitarian Assistance Office), and had been, it was later revealed, carrying cash to and from Central America for Oliver North.

This was, as described, a small world, and one in which encounters seemed at once random and fated, as in the waking dream that was Miami itself. People in this world spoke of having "tripped into an organization." People saw freedom fighters on "Nightline," and then in Miami. People saw boxes in motel rooms, and concluded that the boxes contained C-4. People received telephone calls from strangers, and picked them up at the airport at three in the morning, and began looking for a private plane to fly to Central America. Some people just turned up out of the nowhere: Jesus Garcia happened to meet Thomas Posey because he was working the afternoon shift at the Dade County jail on the day Thomas Posey was booked for trying to take a .380 automatic pistol through the X-ray machine on Concourse G at the Miami airport. Some people turned up not exactly out of the nowhere but all over the map: Jesus Garcia said that he had seen Robert Owen in Miami, more specifically, as an assistant U.S. attorney in Miami put it, "at that Howard Johnson's when they were planning that stuff," by which the assistant U.S. attorney meant weapons flights. Steven Carr said that he had seen Robert Owen in Costa Rica, witnessing a weapons delivery at the base near the Nicaraguan border. Robert Owen, when he eventually appeared before the select committees, acknowledged that he had been present when such a delivery was made, but said that he never saw the actual unloading, and that his presence on the scene was, as the *Miami Herald* put it, "merely coincidental": another random but fated encounter.

There were no particularly novel elements in either the story told by Jesus Garcia or the story told by Steven Carr. They were Miami stories, fragments of the underwater narrative, and as such they were of a genre familiar in this country since at least the Bay of Pigs. Such stories had often been, like these, intrinsically impossible to corroborate. Such stories had often been of doubtful provenance, had been either leaked by prosecutors unable to make a case or elicited, like these, in jailhouse interviews, a circumstance that has traditionally tended, like a DEATH BEFORE DISHONOR tattoo, to work against the credibility of the teller. Any single Miami story, moreover, was hard to follow, and typically required a more extensive recall of other Miami stories than most people outside Miami could offer. Characters would frequently reappear. A convicted bomber named Hector Cornillot, a onetime member of Orlando Bosch's Cuban Power movement, turned out, for example, to have been during the spring of 1985 the night bookkeeper at the Howard Johnson's near the Miami airport. Motivation, often opaque in a first or second appearance, might come clear only in a third, or a tenth.

Miami stories were low, and lurid, and so radically reliant on the inductive leap that they tended to attract advocates of an ideological or paranoid bent, which was another reason they remained, for many people, easy to dismiss. Stories like these had been told to the Warren Commission in 1964, but many people had preferred to discuss what was then called the climate of violence, and the healing process. Stories like these had been told during the Watergate investigations in 1974, but the president had resigned, enabling the healing process, it was again said, to begin. Stories like these had been told to the Church committee in 1975 and 1976, and to the House Select Committee on Assassinations in 1977 and 1978, but many people had preferred to focus instead on the constitutional questions raised, not on the hypodermic syringe containing Black Leaf 40 with which the CIA was trying in November of 1963 to get Fidel Castro assas-

sinated, not on Johnny Roselli in the oil drum in Biscayne Bay, not on that motel room in Dallas where Marita
Lorenz claimed she had seen the rifles and the scopes and
Frank Sturgis and Orlando Bosch and Jack Ruby and the
Novo brothers, but on the separation of powers, and the
proper role of congressional oversight. "The search for
conspiracy," Anthony Lewis had written in *The New York
Times* in September of 1975, "only increases the elements
of morbidity and paranoia and fantasy in this country. It
romanticizes crimes that are terrible because of their lack
of purpose. It obscures our necessary understanding, all of
us, that in this life there is often tragedy without reason."

This was not at the time an uncommon note, nor was
it later. Particularly in Washington, where the logical consequences of any administration's imperial yearnings were
thought to be voided when the voting levers were next
pulled, the study of the underwater narrative, these stories about what people in Miami may or may not have
done on the basis of what people in Washington had or
had not said, was believed to serve no useful purpose. That
the assassination of John F. Kennedy might or might not
have been the specific consequence of his administration's
own incursions into the tropic of morbidity and paranoia
and fantasy (as early as 1964, two staff attorneys for the
Warren Commission, W. David Slawson and William
Coleman, had prepared a memorandum urging the commission to investigate the possibility that Lee Harvey
Oswald had been acting for, or had been set up by, anti-
Castro Cuban exiles) did not recommend, in this view, a
closer study of the tropic. That there might or might not
be, in the wreckage of the Reagan administration, certain

consequences to that administration's similar incursions recommended only, in this view, that it was again time to focus on the mechanical model, time to talk about runaway agencies, arrogance in the executive branch, about constitutional crises and the nature of the presidency, about faults in the structure, flaws in the process; time to talk, above all, about 1988, when the levers would again be pulled and the consequences voided and any lingering morbidity dispelled by the enthusiasms, the energies, of the new team. "Dick Goodwin was handling Latin America and a dozen other problems," Arthur M. Schlesinger, Jr., once told us about the early months of the Kennedy administration, as suggestive a sentence as has perhaps been written about this tabula rasa effect in Washington life.

In the late summer of 1985, some months after the Outreach meeting in Room 450 of the Old Executive Office Building in Washington at which I had heard Jack Wheeler talk about the necessity for supporting freedom fighters around the world, I happened to receive a letter ("Dear Fellow American") from Major General John K. Singlaub, an invitation to the International Freedom Fighters Dinner to be held that September in the Crystal Ballroom of the Registry Hotel in Dallas. This letter was dated August 7, 1985, a date on which Steven Carr was already sitting in La Reforma prison in San José and on which Jesus Garcia was one day short of receiving a call from a twenty-nine-year-old stranger who identified himself as Allen Saum, who said that he was a major in the

U.S. Marines and had been sent by the White House, who enlisted Jesus Garcia in a mission he described as "George Bush's baby," and who then telephoned the Miami office of the FBI and told them where they could pick up Jesus Garcia and his MAC-10. "He looked typical Ivy League, I thought he must be CIA," Jesus Garcia later said about "Allen Saum," who did not show up for Jesus Garcia's trial but did appear at a pretrial hearing, where he said that he took orders from a man he knew only as "Sam."

The letter from General Singlaub urged that any recipient unable to attend the Dallas dinner ($500 a plate) plan in any case to have his or her name listed on the International Freedom Fighters Commemorative Program ($50 a copy), which General Singlaub would, in turn, "personally present to President Reagan." Even the smallest donation, General Singlaub stressed, would go far toward keeping "freedom's light burning." The mujahideen in Afghanistan, for example, who would be among the freedom fighters to benefit from the Dallas dinner (along with those in Angola, Laos, South Vietnam, Cambodia, Mozambique, Ethiopia, and of course Nicaragua), had not long before destroyed "approximately twenty-five per cent of the Afghan government's Soviet supplied air force" (or, according to General Singlaub, twenty MIGs, worth $100 million) with just "a few hundred dollars spent on plastic explosives."

I recall experiencing, as I read this sentence about the mujahideen and the few hundred dollars spent on plastic explosives, the exact sense of expanding, or contracting,

possibility that I had recently experienced during flights
to Miami. Many apparently disparate elements seemed to
be converging in the letter from General Singlaub, and the
convergence was not one that discouraged that "search
for conspiracy" deplored by Anthony Lewis a decade
before. The narrative in which a few hundred dollars
spent on plastic explosives could reverse history, which
appeared to be the scenario on which General Singlaub
and many of the people I had seen in Room 450 were
operating, was the same narrative in which meetings at
private houses in Miami Beach had been seen to overturn
governments. This was that narrative in which the actions
of individuals had been seen to affect events directly, in
which revolutions and counterrevolutions had been framed
in the private sector; that narrative in which the state
security apparatus existed to be enlisted by one or another
private player.

This was also the narrative in which words had tended
to have consequences, and stories endings. NICARAGUA
HOY, CUBA MAÑANA. When Jesus Garcia talked about meeting in the cocktail lounge of the Howard Johnson's near
the Miami airport to discuss a plan to assassinate the
American ambassador to Costa Rica, bomb the American embassy there, and blame it on the Sandinistas, the
American ambassador he was talking about was Lewis
Tambs, one of the authors of the Santa Fe document, the
fifty-three pages that had articulated for many people in
Washington the reasons for the exact American involvement in the politics of the Caribbean that this plan discussed in the cocktail lounge of the Howard Johnson's

near the Miami airport was meant to ensure. Let me tell you about Cuban terrorists, Raúl Rodríguez had said at the midnight dinner in the Arquitectonica condominium overlooking Biscayne Bay. Cuba never grew plastique. Cuba grew tobacco, Cuba grew sugarcane. Cuba never grew C-4.

The air that evening in Miami had been warm and soft even at midnight, and the glass doors had been open onto the terrace overlooking the bay. The daughter of the fifteenth president of the Republic of Cuba, María Elena Prío Durán, whose father's grave at Woodlawn Park Cemetery in Miami lay within sight of the private crypt to which the body of another exiled president, Anastasio Somoza Debayle of Nicaragua, was flown forty-eight hours after his assassination in Asunción (no name on this crypt, no dates, no epitaph, only the monogram "AS" worked among the lilies on a stained-glass window, as if the occupant had negotiated himself out of history), had lit her cigarette and immediately put it out. When Raúl Rodríguez said that evening that C-4 grew here, he was talking about what it had cost to forget that decisions made in Washington had effects outside Washington; about the reverberative effect of certain ideas, and about their consequences. This dinner in Miami took place on March 26, 1985. The meetings in Miami described by Jesus Garcia had already taken place. The flights out of Miami described by Jesus Garcia and Steven Carr had already taken place. These meetings and these flights were the least of what had already taken place; of what was to take place; and also of what, in this world where stories have tended to have endings, has yet to take place. "As a matter of fact I was very definitely involved in the decisions about support to the freedom fighters," the fortieth President of the United States said more than two years later, on May 15, 1987. "My idea to begin with."

—1987

IN THE REALM OF THE
FISHER KING

President Ronald Reagan, we were later told by his speechwriter Peggy Noonan, spent his off-camera time in the White House answering fifty letters a week, selected by the people who ran his mail operation, from citizens. He put the family pictures these citizens sent him in his pockets and desk drawers. When he did not have the zip code, he apologized to his secretary for not looking it up himself. He sharpened his own pencils, we were told by Helene von Damm, his secretary first in Sacramento and then in Washington, and he also got his own coffee.

In the post-Reagan rush to establish that we knew all along about this peculiarity in that particular White House, we forgot the actual peculiarity of the place, which had to do less with the absence at the center than with the amount of centrifugal energy this absence left spinning free at the edges. The Reagan White House was one in which great expectations were allowed into play. Ardor, of a kind that only rarely survives a fully occupied Oval Office, flourished unchecked. "You'd be in someone's home and on the way to the bathroom you'd pass the bedroom and see a big thick copy of Paul Johnson's *Modern Times* lying half open on the table by the bed," Peggy Noonan, who gave Ronald Reagan the boys of Pointe du Hoc and the *Challenger* crew slipping the surly bonds of earth and who gave George Bush the thousand points of light and the kinder, gentler nation, told us in *What I Saw at the Revolution: A Political Life in the Reagan Era.*

"Three months later you'd go back and it was still there," she wrote. "There were words. You had a notion instead of a thought and a dustup instead of a fight, you had a can-do attitude and you were in touch with the zeitgeist. No one had intentions they had an agenda and no one was wrong they were fundamentally wrong and you didn't work on something you broke your pick on it and it wasn't an agreement it was a done deal. All politics is local but more to the point all economics is micro. There were phrases: personnel is policy and ideas have consequences and ideas drive politics and it's a war of ideas . . . and to do nothing is to endorse the status quo and roll back the Brezhnev Doctrine and there's no such thing as a free lunch, especially if you're dining with the press."

Peggy Noonan arrived in Washington in 1984, thirty-three years old, out of Brooklyn and Massapequa and Fairleigh Dickinson and CBS Radio, where she had written Dan Rather's five-minute commentaries. A few years later, when Rather told her that in lieu of a Christmas present he wanted to make a donation to her favorite charity, the charity she specified was The William J. Casey Fund for the Nicaraguan Resistance. She did not immediately, or for some months after, meet the man for whose every public utterance she and the other staff writers were responsible; at the time she checked into the White House, no speechwriter had spoken to Mr. Reagan in more than a year. "We wave to him," one said.

In the absence of an actual president, this resourceful child of a large Irish Catholic family sat in her office in the Old Executive Office Building and invented an ideal one: she read Vachel Lindsay (particularly "I brag and chant of Bryan Bryan Bryan / Candidate for President who sketched a silver Zion") and she read Franklin Delano Roosevelt (whom she pictured, again ideally, up in Dutchess County "sitting at a great table with all the chicks, eating a big spring lunch of beefy red tomatoes and potato salad and mayonnaise and deviled eggs on the old china with the flowers almost rubbed off") and she thought "this is how Reagan should sound." What Miss Noonan had expected Washington to be, she told us, was "Aaron Copland and 'Appalachian Spring.'" What she found instead was a populist revolution trying to make itself, a crisis of raised expectations and lowered possibilities, the children of an expanded middle class determined to tear down the established order and what they saw as its repressive liberal orthodoxies: "There were libertarians whose girlfriends had just given birth to their sons, hoisting a Coors with social conservatives who walked into the party with a wife who bothered to be warm and a son who carried a Mason jar of something daddy grew in the backyard. There were Protestant fundamentalists hoping they wouldn't be dismissed by neo-con intellectuals from Queens and neocons talking to fundamentalists thinking: I wonder if when they look at me they see what Annie Hall's grandmother saw when she looked down the table at Woody Allen."

She stayed at the White House until the spring of 1986, when she was more or less forced out by the refusal of Donald Regan, at that time chief of staff, to approve her promotion to head speechwriter. Regan thought her, according to Larry Speakes, who did not have a famous feel for the romance of the revolution, too "hard-line," too "dogmatic," too "right-wing," too much "Buchanan's protégée." On the occasion of her resignation she received a form letter from the president, signed with the auto-pen. Donald Regan said that there was no need for her to have what was referred to as "a good-bye moment," a farewell shake-hands with the president. On the day Donald Regan himself left the White House, Miss Noonan received this message, left on her answering machine by a friend at the White House: "Hey, Peggy, Don Regan didn't get his good-bye moment." By that time she was hearing the "true tone of Washington" less as "Appalachian Spring" than as something a little more raucous, "nearer," she said, "to Jefferson Starship and 'They Built This City on Rock and Roll.'"

The White House she rendered was one of consider-able febrility. Everyone, she told us, could quote Richard John Neuhaus on what was called the collapse of the dogmas of the secular enlightenment. Everyone could quote Michael Novak on what was called the collapse of the assumption that education is or should be "value-free." Everyone could quote George Gilder on what was called the humane nature of the free market. Everyone could quote Jean-François Revel on how democracies perish, and everyone could quote Jeane Kirkpatrick on authoritarian versus totalitarian governments, and everyone spoke of "the movement," as in "he's movement from way back," or "she's good, she's hard-core."

They talked about subverting the pragmatists, who believed that an issue could not be won without the *Washington Post* and the networks, by "going over the heads of the media to the people." They charged one another's zeal by firing off endless letters, memos, clippings. "Many thanks for Macedo's new monograph; his brand of judicial activism is more principled than Tribe's," such letters read. "If this gets into the hands of the Russians, it's curtains for the free world!" was the tone to take on the yellow Post-It attached to a clipping. "Soldier on!" was the way to sign off. Those PROF memos we later saw from Robert McFarlane to Lieutenant Colonel Oliver North ("Roger Ollie. Well done—if the world only knew how many times you have kept a semblance of integrity and gumption to US policy, they would make you Secretary of State. But they can't know and would complain if they did—such is the state of democracy in the late 20th century. . . . Bravo Zulu") do not seem, in this context, quite so unusual.

"Bureaucrats with soft hands adopted the clipped laconic style of John Ford characters," Miss Noonan noted. "A small man from NSC was asked at a meeting if he knew of someone who could work up a statement. Yes, he knew someone at State, a paid pen who's pushed some good paper." To be a moderate was to be a "squish," or a "weenie," or a "wuss." "He got rolled," they would say of someone who had lost the day, or, "He took a lickin' and kept on tickin'." They walked around the White House wearing ties ("slightly stained," according to Miss Noonan, "from the mayonnaise that fell from the sandwich that was wolfed down at the working lunch on judicial reform") embroidered with the code of the movement: eagles, flags, busts of Jefferson. Little gold Laffer curves identified the wearers as "free-market purists." Liberty bells stood for "judicial restraint."

The favored style here, like the favored foreign policy, seems to have been less military than paramilitary, a matter of talking tough. "That's not off my disk," Lieutenant Colonel Oliver North would snap by way of indicating that an idea was not his. "The fellas," as Miss Noonan called them, the sharp, the smooth, the inner circle and those who aspired to it, made a point of not using seat belts on Air Force One. The less smooth flaunted souvenirs of action on the far borders of the Reagan doctrine. "Jack Wheeler came back from Afghanistan with a Russian officer's belt slung over his shoulder," Miss Noonan recalls. "Grover Norquist came back from Africa rubbing his eyes from taking notes in a tent with Savimbi." Miss Noonan herself had lunch in the White House mess with a "mujahideen warrior" and his public relations man. "What is the condition of your troops in the field?" she asked. "We need help," he said. The Filipino steward approached, pad and pencil in hand. The mujahideen leader looked up. "I will have meat," he said.

This is not a milieu in which one readily places Nancy
Reagan, whose preferred style derived from the more
structured, if equally rigorous, world from which she had
come. The nature of this world was not very well understood. I recall being puzzled, on visits to Washington during the first year or two of the Reagan administration, by
the tenacity of certain misapprehensions about the Reagans and the men generally regarded as their intimates,
that small group of industrialists and entrepreneurs who
had encouraged and financed, as a venture in risk capital,
Ronald Reagan's appearances in both Sacramento and
Washington. The president was above all, I was told repeatedly, a Californian, a Westerner, as were the acquaintances
who made up his kitchen cabinet; it was the "Westernness" of these men that explained not only their rather
intransigent views about America's mission in the world
but also their apparent lack of interest in or identification
with Americans for whom the trend was less reliably up.
It was "Westernness," too, that could explain those affronts
to the local style so discussed in Washington during the
early years, the overwrought clothes and the borrowed jew-
elry and the Le Cirque hair and the wall-to-wall carpeting
and the table settings. In style and substance alike, the Reagans and their friends were said to display what was first
called "the California mentality," and then, as the administration got more settled and the social demonology of
the exotic landscape more specific, "the California Club
mentality."

I recall hearing about this "California Club mentality"

at a dinner table in Georgetown, and responding with a certain atavistic outrage (I was from California, my own brother then lived during the week at the California Club); what seems curious in retrospect is that many of the men in question, including the president, had only a convenient connection with California in particular and the West in general. William Wilson was actually born in Los Angeles, and Earle Jorgenson in San Francisco, but the late Justin Dart was born in Illinois, graduated from Northwestern, married a Walgreen heiress in Chicago, and did not move United Rexall, later Dart Industries, from Boston to Los Angeles until he was already its president. The late Alfred Bloomingdale was born in New York, graduated from Brown, and seeded the Diners Club with money from his family's New York store. What these men represented was not "the West" but what was for this century a relatively new kind of monied class in America, a group devoid of social responsibilities precisely because their ties to any one place had been so attenuated.

Ronald and Nancy Reagan had in fact lived most of their adult lives in California, but as part of the entertainment community, the members of which do not belong to the California Club. In 1964, when I first went to live in Los Angeles, and for some years later, life in the upper reaches of this community was, for women, quite rigidly organized. Women left the table after dessert, and had coffee upstairs, isolated in the bedroom or dressing room with demitasse cups and rock sugar ordered from London and cinnamon sticks in lieu of demitasse spoons. On the hostess's dressing table there were always very large bottles of Fracas and Gardenia and Tuberose. The dessert that preceded this retreat (a soufflé or mousse with raspberry sauce) was inflexibly served on Flora Danica plates, and was itself preceded by the ritual of the finger bowls and the doilies. I recall being repeatedly told a cautionary tale about what Joan Crawford had said to a young woman who removed her finger bowl but left the doily. The details of exactly what Joan Crawford had said and to whom and at whose table she had said it differed with the teller, but it was always Joan Crawford, and it always involved the doily; one of the reasons Mrs. Reagan ordered the famous new china was because, she told us in her own account of life in the Reagan White House, *My Turn,* the Johnson china had no finger bowls.

These subtropical evenings were not designed to invigorate. Large arrangements of flowers, ordered from David Jones, discouraged attempts at general conversation, ensuring that the table was turned on schedule. Expensive "resort" dresses and pajamas were worn, Pucci silks to the floor. When the women rejoined the men downstairs, trays of white crème de menthe were passed. Large parties were held in tents, with pink lights and chili from Chasen's. Lunch took place at the Bistro, and later at the Bistro Garden and at Jimmy's, which was owned by Jimmy Murphy, who everyone knew because he had worked for Kurt Niklas at the Bistro.

These forms were those of the local *ancien régime,* and as such had largely faded out by the late sixties, but can be examined in detail in the photographs Jean Howard took over the years and collected in *Jean Howard's Hollywood: A Photo Memoir*. Although neither Reagan appears in Miss Howard's book (the people she saw tended to be stars or powers or famously amusing, and the Reagans, who fell into hard times and television, were not locally thought to fill any of these slots), the photographs give a sense of the rigors of the place. What one notices in a photograph of the Joseph Cottens' 1955 Fourth of July lunch, the day Jennifer Jones led the conga line into the pool, is not the pool. There are people in the pool, yes, and even chairs, but most of the guests sit decorously on the lawn, wearing rep ties, silk dresses, high-heeled shoes. Mrs. Henry Hathaway, for a day in the sun at Anatole Litvak's beach house, wears a strapless dress of embroidered and scalloped organdy, and pearl earrings. Natalie Wood, lunching on Minna Wallis's lawn with Warren Beatty and George Cukor and the Hathaways and the Minnellis and the Axelrods, wears a black straw hat with a silk ribbon, a white dress, black and white beads, perfect full makeup, and her hair pinned back.

This was the world from which Nancy Reagan went in 1966 to Sacramento and in 1980 to Washington, and it is in many ways the world, although it was vanishing *in situ* even before Ronald Reagan was elected governor of California, she never left. *My Turn* did not document a life radically altered by later experience. Eight years in Sacramento left so little imprint on Mrs. Reagan that she described the house in which she lived there—a house located on 45th Street off M Street in a city laid out on a numerical and alphabetical grid running from 1st Street to 66th Street and from A Street to Y Street—as "an English-style country house in the suburbs."

She did not find it unusual that this house should have been bought for and rented to her and her husband (they paid $1,250 a month) by the same group of men who gave the State of California eleven acres on which to build Mrs. Reagan the "governor's mansion" she actually wanted and who later funded the million-dollar redecoration of the Reagan White House and who eventually bought the house on St. Cloud Road in Bel Air to which the Reagans moved when they left Washington (the street number of the St. Cloud house was 666, but the Reagans had it changed to 668, to avoid an association with the Beast in Revelations); she seemed to construe houses as part of her deal, like the housing provided to actors on location. Before the kitchen cabinet picked up Ronald Reagan's contract, the Reagans had lived in a house in Pacific Palisades remodeled by his then sponsor, General Electric.

This expectation on the part of the Reagans that other people would care for their needs struck many people, right away, as remarkable, and was usually characterized as a habit of the rich. But of course it is not a habit of the rich, and in any case the Reagans were not rich: they, and this expectation, were the products of studio Hollywood, a system in which performers performed, and in return were cared for. "I preferred the studio system to the anxiety of looking for work in New York," Mrs. Reagan told us in *My Turn*. During the eight years she lived in Washington, Mrs. Reagan said, she "never once set foot in a supermarket or in almost any other kind of store, with the exception of a card shop at 17th and K, where I used to buy my birthday cards," and carried money only when she went out for a manicure.

She was surprised to learn ("Nobody had told us") that she and her husband were expected to pay for their own food, dry cleaning, and toothpaste while in the White House. She seemed never to understand why it was imprudent of her to have accepted clothes from their makers when so many of them encouraged her to do so. Only Geoffrey Beene, whose clothes for Patricia Nixon and whose wedding dress for Lynda Bird Johnson were purchased through stores at retail prices, seemed to have resisted this impulse. "I don't quite understand how clothes can be 'on loan' to a woman," he told the *Los Angeles Times* in January of 1982, when the question of Mrs. Reagan's clothes was first raised. "I also think they'll run into a great deal of trouble deciding which of all these clothes are of museum quality. . . . They also claim she's helping to 'rescue' the American fashion industry. I didn't know it was in such dire straits."

The clothes were, as Mrs. Reagan seemed to construe it, "wardrobe"—a production expense, like the housing and the catering and the first-class travel and the furniture and paintings and cars that get taken home after the set is struck—and should rightly have gone on the studio budget. That the producers of this particular production—the men Mrs. Reagan called their "wealthier friends," their "very generous" friends—sometimes misunderstood their own role was understandable: Helene von Damm told us that only after William Wilson was warned that anyone with White House credentials was subject to a full-scale FBI investigation (Fred Fielding, the White House counsel, told him this) did he relinquish Suite 180 of the Executive Office Building, which he had commandeered the day after the inauguration in order to vet the appointment of the nominal, as opposed to the kitchen, cabinet.

"So began my stewardship," Edith Bolling Wilson wrote later about the stroke that paralyzed Woodrow Wilson in October of 1919, eighteen months before he left the White House. The stewardship Nancy Reagan shared first with James Baker and Ed Meese and Michael Deaver and then less easily with Donald Regan was, perhaps because each of its principals was working a different scenario and only one, James Baker, had anything approaching a full script, considerably more Byzantine than most. Baker, whose ultimate role in this White House was to preserve it for the established order, seems to have relied heavily on the tendency of opposing forces, let loose, to neutralize each other. "Usually in a big place there's only one person or group to be afraid of," Peggy Noonan observed. "But in the Reagan White House there were two, the chief of staff and his people and the First Lady and hers—a pincer formation that made everyone feel vulnerable." Miss Noonan showed us Mrs. Reagan moving through the corridors with her East Wing entourage, the members of which were said in the West Wing to be "not serious," readers of *W* and *Vogue*. Mrs. Reagan herself was variously referred to as "Evita," "Mommy," "The Missus," "The Hairdo with Anxiety." Miss Noonan dismissed her as not "a liberal or a leftist or a moderate or a détentist" but "a Galanoist, a wealthy well-dressed woman who followed the common wisdom of her class."

In fact Nancy Reagan was more interesting than that: it was precisely "her class" in which she had trouble believing. She was not an experienced woman. Her social skills, like those of many women trained in the insular life of the motion picture community, were strikingly undeveloped. She and Raisa Gorbachev had "little in common," and "completely different outlooks on the world." She and Betty Ford "were different people who came from different worlds." She seems to have been comfortable in the company of Michael Deaver, of Ted Graber (her decorator), and of only a few other people. She seems not to have had much sense about who goes with who. At a state dinner for José Napoleón Duarte of El Salvador, she seated herself between President Duarte and Ralph Lauren. She had limited social experience and apparently unlimited social anxiety. Helene von Damm complained that Mrs. Reagan would not consent, during the first presidential campaign, to letting the fund-raisers call on "her New York friends"; trying to put together a list for the New York dinner in November of 1979 at which Ronald Reagan was to announce his candidacy, Miss von Damm finally dispatched an emissary to extract a few names from Jerry Zipkin, who parted with them reluctantly, and then said, "Remember, don't use my name."

Perhaps Mrs. Reagan's most endearing quality was this little girl's fear of being left out, of not having the best friends and not going to the parties in the biggest houses. She collected slights. She took refuge in a kind of piss-elegance, a fanciness (the "English-style country house in the suburbs"), in using words like "inappropriate." It was "inappropriate, to say the least" for Geraldine Ferraro and her husband to leave the dais and go "down on the floor, working the crowd" at a 1984 Italian-American Federation dinner at which the candidates on both tickets were speaking. It was "uncalled for—and mean" when, at the time John Koehler had been named to replace Patrick Buchanan as director of communications and it was learned that Koehler had been a member of Hitler Youth, Donald Regan said "blame it on the East Wing."

Mrs. Gorbachev, as Mrs. Reagan saw it, "condescended" to her, and "expected to be deferred to." Mrs. Gorbachev accepted an invitation from Pamela Harriman before she answered one from Mrs. Reagan. The reason Ben Bradlee called Iran-contra "the most fun he'd had since Watergate" was just possibly because, she explained in *My Turn,* he resented her relationship with Katharine Graham. Betty Ford was given a box on the floor of the 1976 Republican National Convention, and Mrs. Reagan only a skybox. Mrs. Reagan was evenhanded: Maureen Reagan "may have been right" when she called this slight deliberate. When, on the second night of that convention, the band struck up "Tie a Yellow Ribbon Round the Ole Oak Tree" during an ovation for Mrs. Reagan, Mrs. Ford started dancing with Tony Orlando. Mrs. Reagan was magnanimous: "Some of our people saw this as a deliberate attempt to upstage me, but I never thought that was her intention."

Michael Deaver, in his version of more or less the same events, *Behind the Scenes,* gave us an arresting account of taking the Reagans, during the 1980 campaign, to an Episcopal church near the farm on which they were staying outside Middleburg, Virginia. After advancing the church and negotiating the subject of the sermon with the minister (Ezekiel and the bones rather than what Deaver called "reborn Christians," presumably Christian rebirth), he finally agreed that the Reagans would attend an eleven o'clock Sunday service. "We were not told," Deaver wrote, "and I did not anticipate, that the eleven o'clock service would also be holy communion," a ritual he characterized as "very foreign to the Reagans." He described "nervous glances," and "mildly frantic" whispers about what to do, since the Reagans' experience had been of Bel Air Presbyterian, "a proper Protestant church where trays are passed containing small glasses of grape juice and little squares of bread." The moment arrived: ". . . halfway down the aisle I felt Nancy clutch my arm. . . . *'Mike!'* she hissed. *'Are those people drinking out of the same cup?'"*

Here the incident takes on elements of *I Love Lucy.* Deaver assures Mrs. Reagan that it will be acceptable to just dip the wafer in the chalice. Mrs. Reagan chances this, but manages somehow to drop the wafer in the wine. Ronald Reagan, cast here as Ricky Ricardo, is too deaf to hear Deaver's whispered instructions, and has been instructed by his wife to "do exactly as I do." He, too, drops the wafer in the wine, where it is left to float next to Mrs. Reagan's. "Nancy was relieved to leave the church," Deaver reports. "The president was chipper as he stepped into the sunlight, satisfied that the service had gone quite well."

I had read this account several times before I realized what so attracted me to it: here we had a perfect model of the Reagan White House. There was the aide who located the correct setting ("I did some quick scouting and found a beautiful Episcopal church"), who anticipated every conceivable problem and handled it adroitly (he had "a discreet chat with the minister," and he "gently raised the question"), and yet who somehow missed, as in the visit to Bitburg, a key point. There was the wife, charged with protecting her husband's face to the world, a task requiring, she hinted in *My Turn,* considerable vigilance. This was a husband who could be "naive about people." He had, for example, "too much trust" in David Stockman. He had "given his word" to Helmut Kohl, and so felt "duty-bound to honor his commitment" to visit Bitburg. He was, Mrs. Reagan disclosed during a "Good Morning America" interview at the time *My Turn* was published, "the softest touch going" when it came to what she referred to as (another instance of somehow missing a key point) "the poor." Mrs. Reagan understood all this. She handled all this. And yet there she was outside Middleburg, Virginia, once again the victim of bad advance, confronted by the "foreign" communion table and rendered stiff with apprehension that a finger bowl might get removed without its doily.

And there, at the center of it all, was Ronald Reagan, insufficiently briefed (or, as they say in the White House, "badly served") on the wafer issue but moving ahead, stepping "into the sunlight" satisfied with his own and everyone else's performance, apparently oblivious of (or inured to, or indifferent to) the crises being managed in his presence and for his benefit. What he had, and the aide and the wife did not have, was the story, the high concept, what Ed Meese used to call "the big picture," as in "he's a big-picture man." The big picture here was of the candidate going to church on Sunday morning; the details obsessing the wife and the aide—what church, what to do with the wafer—remained outside the frame.

From the beginning in California, the principal in this administration was operating on what might have seemed distinctly special information. He had "feelings" about things; for example, about the Vietnam War. "I have a feeling that we are doing better in the war than the people have been told," he was quoted as having said in the *Los Angeles Times* on October 16, 1967. With the transforming power of the presidency, this special information that no one else understood—these big pictures, these high concepts—took on a magical quality, and some people in the White House came to believe that they had in their possession, sharpening his own pencils in the Oval Office, the Fisher King himself, the keeper of the grail, the source of that ineffable contact with the electorate that was in turn the source of the power.

There were times, we know now, when this White House had fairly well absented itself from the art of the possible. McFarlane flying to Teheran with the cake and the Bible and ten falsified Irish passports did not derive from our traditional executive tradition. The place was running instead on its own superstition, on the reading of bones, on the belief that a flicker of attention from the president during the presentation of a plan (the ideal presentation, Peggy Noonan explained, was one in which "the president was forced to look at a picture, read a short letter, or respond to a question") ensured the transfer of the magic to whatever was that week exciting the ardor of the children who wanted to make the revolution—to SDI, to the mujahadeen, to Jonas Savimbi, to the contras.

Miss Noonan recalled what she referred to as "the contra meetings," which turned on the magical notion that putting the president on display in the right setting (i.e., "going over the heads of the media to the people") was all that was needed to "inspire a commitment on the part of the American people." They sat in those meetings and discussed having the president speak at the Orange Bowl in Miami on the anniversary of John F. Kennedy's Orange Bowl speech after the Bay of Pigs, never mind that the Kennedy Orange Bowl speech had become over the years in Miami the symbol of American betrayal. They sat in those meetings and discussed having the president go over the heads of his congressional opponents by speaking in Jim Wright's district near the Alamo: ." . . something like 'Blank miles to the north of here is the Alamo,'" Miss Noonan wrote in her notebook, sketching out the ritual in which the magic would be transferred. "'. . . Where brave heroes blank, and where the commander of the garrison wrote during those terrible last days blank . . .'"

But the Fisher King was sketching another big picture, one he had had in mind since California. We have heard again and again that Mrs. Reagan turned the president away from the Evil Empire and toward the meetings with Gorbachev. (Later, on NBC "Nightly News," the San Francisco astrologer Joan Quigley claimed a role in influencing both Reagans on this point, explaining that she had "changed their Evil Empire attitude by briefing them on Gorbachev's horoscope.") Mrs. Reagan herself allowed that she "felt it was ridiculous for these two heavily armed superpowers to be sitting there and not talking to each other" and "did push Ronnie a little."

But how much pushing was actually needed remains in question. The Soviet Union appeared to Ronald Reagan as an abstraction, a place where people were helpless to resist "communism," the inanimate evil that, as he had put it in a 1951 speech to a Kiwanis convention and would continue to put it for the next three and a half decades, had "tried to invade our industry" and been "fought" and eventually "licked." This was a construct in which the actual citizens of the Soviet Union could be seen to have been, like the motion picture industry, "invaded"—in need only of liberation. The liberating force might be the appearance of a Shane-like character, someone to "lick" the evil, or it might be just the sweet light of reason. "A people free to choose will always choose peace," as President Reagan told students at Moscow State University in May of 1988.

In this sense he was dealing from an entirely abstract deck, and the opening to the East had been his card all along, his big picture, his story. And this is how it went: what he would like to do, he had told any number of people over the years (I recall first hearing it from George Will, who cautioned me not to tell it because conversations with presidents were privileged), was take the leader of the Soviet Union (who this leader would be was another of those details outside the frame) on a flight to Los Angeles. When the plane came in low over the middle-class subdivisions that stretch from the San Bernardino mountains to LAX, he would direct the leader of the Soviet Union to the window, and point out all the swimming pools below. "Those are the pools of the capitalists," the leader of the Soviet Union would say. "No," the leader of the free world would say. "Those are the pools of the workers." *Blank* years further on, when brave heroes *blanked,* and where the leader of the free world *blank,* accidental history took its course, but we have yet to pay for the ardor.

—*1989*

SENTIMENTAL JOURNEYS

1

We know her story, and some of us, although not all of us, which was to become one of the story's several equivocal aspects, know her name. She was a twenty-nine-year-old unmarried white woman who worked as an investment banker in the corporate finance department at Salomon Brothers in downtown Manhattan, the energy and natural resources group. She was said by one of the principals in a Texas oil-stock offering on which she had collaborated as a member of the Salomon team to have done "top-notch" work. She lived alone in an apartment on East 83rd Street, between York and East End, a sublet cooperative she was thinking about buying. She often worked late and when she got home she would change into jogging clothes and at eight-thirty or nine-thirty in the evening would go running, six or seven miles through Central Park, north on the East Drive, west on the less traveled road connecting the East and West Drives at approximately 102nd Street, and south on the West Drive. The wisdom of this was later questioned by some, by those who were accustomed to thinking of the Park as a place to avoid after dark, and defended by others, the more adroit of whom spoke of the citizen's absolute right to public access ("That park belongs to us and this time nobody is going to take it from us," Ronnie Eldridge, at the time a Democratic candidate for the City Council of New York, declared on the op-ed page of the *New York Times*), others of whom spoke of "running" as a preemptive right. "Runners have Type A controlled personalities and they don't like their schedules interrupted," one runner, a securities trader, told the *Times* to this point. "When people run is a function of their lifestyle," another runner said. "I am personally very angry," a third said. "Because women should have the right to run anytime."

For this woman in this instance these notional rights did not prevail. She was found, with her clothes torn off, not far from the 102nd Street connecting road at one-thirty in the morning of April 20, 1989. She was taken near death to Metropolitan Hospital on East 97th Street. She had lost 75 percent of her blood. Her skull had been crushed, her left eyeball pushed back through its socket, the characteristic surface wrinkles of her brain flattened. Dirt and twigs were found in her vagina, suggesting rape. By May 2, when she first woke from coma, six black and Hispanic teenagers, four of whom had made videotaped statements concerning their roles in the attack and another of whom had described his role in an unsigned verbal statement, had been charged with her assault and rape and she had become, unwilling and unwitting, a sacrificial player in the sentimental narrative that is New York public life.

Nightmare in Central Park, the headlines and display type read. *Teen Wolfpack Beats and Rapes Wall Street Exec on Jogging Path. Central Park Horror. Wolf Pack's Prey. Female Jogger Near Death After Savage Attack by Roving Gang. Rape Rampage. Park Marauders Call It "Wilding," Street Slang for going Berserk. Rape Suspect: "It Was Fun." Rape Suspect's Jailhouse Boast: "She Wasn't Nothing." The teenagers were back in the holding cell, the confessions gory and complete. One shouted "hit the beat" and they all started rapping to "Wild Thing." The Jogger and the Wolf Pack. An Outrage and a Prayer.* And, on the Monday morning after the attack, on the front page of the *New York Post,* with a photograph of Governor Mario Cuomo and the headline *"None of Us Is Safe,"* this italic text: "A visibly shaken Governor Cuomo spoke out yesterday on the vicious Central Park rape: 'The people are angry and frightened—my mother is, my family is. To me, as a person who's lived in this city all of his life, this is the ultimate shriek of alarm.'"

Later it would be recalled that 3,254 other rapes were reported that year, including one the following week involving the near decapitation of a black woman in Fort Tryon Park and one two weeks later involving a black woman in Brooklyn who was robbed, raped, sodomized, and thrown down an air shaft of a four-story building, but the point was rhetorical, since crimes are universally understood to be news to the extent that they offer, however erroneously, a story, a lesson, a high concept. In the 1986 Central Park death of Jennifer Levin, then eighteen, at the hands of Robert Chambers, then nineteen, the "story," extrapolated more or less from thin air but left largely uncorrected, had to do not with people living wretchedly and marginally on the underside of where they wanted to be, not with the Dreiserian pursuit of "respectability" that marked the revealed details (Robert Chambers's mother was a private-duty nurse who worked twelve-hour night shifts to enroll her son in private schools and the Knickerbocker Greys), but with "preppies," and the familiar "too much too soon."

Susan Brownmiller, during a year spent monitoring newspaper coverage of rape as part of her research for *Against Our Will: Men, Women and Rape,* found, not surprisingly, that "although New York City police statistics showed that black women were more frequent victims of rape than white women, the favored victim in the tabloid headline . . . was young, white, middle class and 'attractive.'" In its quite extensive coverage of rape-murders during the year 1971, according to Ms. Brownmiller, the *Daily News* published in its four-star final edition only two stories in which the victim was not described in the lead paragraph as "attractive": one of these stories involved an eight-year-old child, the other was a second-day follow-up on a first-day story that had in fact described the victim as "attractive." The *Times,* she found, covered rapes only infrequently that year, but what coverage they did "concerned victims who had some kind of middle-class status, such as 'nurse,' 'dancer' or 'teacher,' and with a favored setting of Central Park."

As a news story, "Jogger" was understood to turn on the demonstrable "difference" between the victim and her accused assailants, four of whom lived in Schomburg Plaza, a federally subsidized apartment complex at the northeast corner of Fifth Avenue and 110th Street in East Harlem, and the rest of whom lived in the projects and rehabilitated tenements just to the north and west of Schomburg Plaza. Some twenty-five teenagers were brought in for questioning; eight were held. The six who were finally indicted ranged in age from fourteen to sixteen. That none of the six had previous police records passed, in this context, for achievement; beyond that, one was recalled by his classmates to have taken pride in his expensive basketball shoes, another to have been "a follower." *I'm a smooth type of fellow, cool, calm, and mellow,* one of the six, Yusef Salaam, would say in the rap he presented as part of his statement before sentencing.

> *I'm kind of laid back, but now I'm speaking so that you know*
> *I got used and abused and even was put on the news. . . .*
> *I'm not dissing them all, but the some that I called.*
> *They tried to dis me like I was an inch small, like a midget, a*
> *mouse, something less than a man.*

The victim, by contrast, was a leader, part of what the *Times* would describe as "the wave of young professionals who took over New York in the 1980s," one of those who were "handsome and pretty and educated and white," who, according to the *Times,* not only "believed they owned the world" but "had reason to." She was from a Pittsburgh suburb, Upper St. Clair, the daughter of a retired Westinghouse senior manager. She had been Phi Beta Kappa at Wellesley, a graduate of the Yale School of

Management, a congressional intern, nominated for a Rhodes Scholarship, remembered by the chairman of her department at Wellesley as "probably one of the top four or five students of the decade." She was reported to be a vegetarian, and "fun-loving," although only "when time permitted," and also to have had (these were the *Times'* details) "concerns about the ethics of the American business world."

In other words she was wrenched, even as she hung between death and life and later between insentience and sentience, into New York's ideal sister, daughter, Bacharach bride: a young woman of conventional middle-class privilege and promise whose situation was such that many people tended to overlook the fact that the state's case against the accused was not invulnerable. The state could implicate most of the defendants in the assault and rape in their own videotaped words, but had none of the incontrovertible forensic evidence—no matching semen, no matching fingernail scrapings, no matching blood—commonly produced in this kind of case. Despite the fact that jurors in the second trial would eventually mention physical evidence as having been crucial in their bringing guilty verdicts against one defendant, Kevin Richardson, there was not actually much physical evidence at hand. Fragments of hair "similar [to] and consistent" with that of the victim were found on Kevin Richardson's clothing and underwear, but the state's own criminologist had testified that hair samples were necessarily inconclusive since, unlike fingerprints, they could not be traced to a single person. Dirt samples found on the defendants' clothing were, again, similar to dirt found in that part of the park where the attack took place, but the state's criminologist allowed that the samples were also similar to dirt found in other uncultivated areas of the park. To suggest, however, that this minimal physical evidence could open the case to an aggressive defense—to, say, the kind of defense that such celebrated New York criminal lawyers as Jack Litman and Barry Slotnick typically present—would come to be construed, during the weeks and months to come, as a further attack on the victim.

She would be Lady Courage to the *New York Post,* she would be A Profile in Courage to the *Daily News* and *New York Newsday.* She would become for Anna Quindlen in the *New York Times* the figure of "New York rising above the dirt, the New Yorker who has known the best, and the worst, and has stayed on, living somewhere in the middle." She would become for David Dinkins, the first black mayor of New York, the emblem of his apparently fragile hopes for the city itself: "I hope the city will be able to learn a lesson from this event and be inspired by the young woman who was assaulted in the case," he said. "Despite tremendous odds, she is rebuilding her life. What a human life can do, a human society can do as well." She was even then for John Gutfreund, at that time the chairman and chief executive officer of Salomon Brothers, the personification of "what makes this city so vibrant and so great," now "struck down by a side of our city that is as awful and terrifying as the creative side is wonderful." It was precisely in this conflation of victim and city, this confusion of personal woe with public distress, that the crime's "story" would be found, its lesson, its encouraging promise of narrative resolution.

One reason the victim in this case could be so readily abstracted, and her situation so readily made to stand for that of the city itself, was that she remained, as a victim of rape, unnamed in most press reports. Although the American and English press convention of not naming victims of rape (adult rape victims are named in French papers) derives from the understandable wish to protect the victim, the rationalization of this special protection rests on a number of doubtful, even magical, assumptions. The convention assumes, by providing a protection for victims of rape not afforded victims of other assaults, that rape involves a violation absent from other kinds of assault. The convention assumes that this violation is of a nature best kept secret, that the rape victim feels, and would feel still more strongly were she identified, a shame and self-loathing unique to this form of assault; in other words that she has been in an unspecified way party to her own assault, that a special contract exists between this one kind of victim and her assailant. The convention assumes, finally, that the victim would be, were this special contract revealed, the natural object of prurient interest; that the act of male penetration involves such potent mysteries that the woman so penetrated (as opposed, say, to having her face crushed with a brick or her brain penetrated with a length of pipe) is permanently marked, "different," even—especially if there is a perceived racial or social "difference" between victim and assailant, as in nineteenth-century stories featuring white women taken by Indians—"ruined."

These quite specifically masculine assumptions (women do not want to be raped, nor do they want to have their brains smashed, but very few mystify the difference between the two) tend in general to be self-fulfilling, guiding the victim to define her assault as her protectors do. "Ultimately we're doing women a disservice by separating rape from other violent crimes," Deni Elliott, the director of Dartmouth's Ethics Institute, suggested in a discussion of this custom in *Time.* "We are participating in the stigma of rape by treating victims of this crime differently," Geneva Overholser, the editor of the *Des Moines Register,* said about her decision to publish in February of 1990 a five-part piece about a rape victim who agreed to be named. "When we as a society refuse to talk openly about rape, I think we weaken our ability to deal with it." Susan Estrich, a professor of criminal law at Harvard Law School and the manager of Michael Dukakis's 1988 presidential campaign, discussed, in *Real Rape,* the conflicting emotions that followed her own 1974 rape:

> At first, being raped is something you simply don't talk about. Then it occurs to you that people whose houses are broken into or who are mugged in Central Park talk about it *all* the time. . . . If it isn't my fault, why am I supposed to be ashamed? If I'm not ashamed, if it wasn't "personal," why look askance when I mention it?

There were, in the 1989 Central Park attack, specific circumstances that reinforced the conviction that the victim should not be named. She had clearly been, according to the doctors who examined her at Metropolitan

Hospital and to the statements made by the suspects (she herself remembered neither the attack nor anything that happened during the next six weeks), raped by one or more assailants. She had also been beaten so brutally that, fifteen months later, she could not focus her eyes or walk unaided. She had lost all sense of smell. She could not read without experiencing double vision. She was believed at the time to have permanently lost function in some areas of her brain.

Given these circumstances, the fact that neither the victim's family nor, later, the victim herself wanted her name known struck an immediate chord of sympathy, seemed a belated way to protect her as she had not been protected in Central Park. Yet there was in this case a special emotional undertow that derived in part from the deep and allusive associations and taboos attaching, in American black history, to the idea of the rape of white women. Rape remained, in the collective memory of many blacks, the very core of their victimization. Black men were accused of raping white women, even as black women were, Malcolm X wrote in *The Autobiography of Malcolm X,* "raped by the slavemaster white man until there had begun to emerge a homemade, handmade, brainwashed race that was no longer even of its true color, that no longer even knew its true family names." The very frequency of sexual contact between white men and black women increased the potency of the taboo on any such contact between black men and white women. The abolition of slavery, W. J. Cash wrote in *The Mind of the South,*

... in destroying the rigid fixity of the black at the bottom of the scale, in throwing open to him at least the legal opportunity to advance, had inevitably opened up to the mind of every Southerner a vista at the end of which stood the overthrow of this taboo. If it was given to the black to advance at all, who could say (once more the logic of the doctrine of his inherent inferiority would not hold) that he would not one day advance the whole way and lay claim to complete equality, including, specifically, the ever crucial right of marriage?

What Southerners felt, therefore, was that any assertion of any kind on the part of the Negro constituted in a perfectly real manner an attack on the Southern woman. What they saw, more or less consciously, in the conditions of Reconstruction was a passage toward a condition for her as degrading, in their view, as rape itself. And a condition, moreover, which, logic or no logic, they infallibly thought of as being as absolutely forced upon her as rape, and hence a condition for which the term "rape" stood as truly as for the *de facto* deed.

Nor was the idea of rape the only potentially treacherous undercurrent in this case. There has historically been, for American blacks, an entire complex of loaded references around the question of "naming": slave names, masters' names, African names, call me by my rightful name, nobody knows my name; stories, in which the specific gravity of naming locked directly into that of rape, of black men whipped for addressing white women by their given names. That, in this case, just such an interlocking of references could work to fuel resentments and inchoate hatreds seemed clear, and it seemed equally clear that some of what ultimately occurred—the repeated references to lynchings, the identification of the defendants with the Scottsboro boys, the insistently provocative repetition of the victim's name, the weird and self-defeating insistence that no rape had taken place and little harm been done the victim—derived momentum from this historical freight. "Years ago, if a white woman said a Black man looked at her lustfully, he could be hung higher than a magnolia tree in bloom, while a white mob watched joyfully sipping tea and eating cookies," Yusef Salaam's mother reminded readers of the *Amsterdam News.* "The first thing you do in the United States of America when a white woman is raped is round up a bunch of black youths, and I think that's what happened here," the Reverend Calvin O. Butts III of the Abyssinian Baptist Church in Harlem told the *New York Times.* "You going to arrest me now because I said the jogger's name?" Gary Byrd asked rhetorically on his WLIB show, and was quoted by Edwin Diamond in *New York* magazine:

> I mean, she's obviously a public figure, and a very mysterious one, I might add. Well, it's a funny place we live in called America, and should we be surprised that they're up to their usual tricks? It was a trick that got us here in the first place.

This reflected one of the problems with not naming this victim: she was in fact named all the time. Everyone in the courthouse, everyone who worked for a paper or a television station or who followed the case for whatever professional reason, knew her name. She was referred to by name in all court records and in all court proceedings. She was named, in the days immediately following the attack, on some local television stations. She was also routinely named—and this was part of the difficulty, part of what led to a damaging self-righteousness among those who did not name her and to an equally damaging embattlement among those who did—in Manhattan's black-owned newspapers, the *Amsterdam News* and the *City Sun,* and she was named as well on WLIB, the Manhattan radio station owned by a black partnership that included Percy Sutton and, until 1985, when he transferred his stock to his son, Mayor Dinkins.

That the victim in this case was identified on Centre Street and north of 96th Street but not in between made for a certain cognitive dissonance, especially since the names of even the juvenile suspects had been released by the police and the press before any suspect had been arraigned, let alone indicted. "The police normally withhold the names of minors who are accused of crimes," the *Times* explained (actually the police normally withhold the names of accused "juveniles," or minors under age sixteen, but not of minors sixteen or seventeen), "but officials said they made public the names of the youths charged in the attack on the woman because of the seriousness of the incident." There seemed a debatable point here, the question of whether "the seriousness of the incident" might not have in fact seemed a compelling reason to avoid any appearance of a rush to judgment by preserving the anonymity of a juvenile suspect; one of the names released by the police and published in the *Times* was of a fourteen-year-old who was ultimately not indicted.

There were, early on, certain aspects of this case that seemed not well handled by the police and prosecutors, and others that seemed not well handled by the press. It would seem to have been tactically unwise, since New York State law requires that a parent or guardian be present when children under sixteen are questioned, for police to continue the interrogation of Yusef Salaam, then fifteen, on the grounds that his Transit Authority bus pass said he was sixteen, while his mother was kept waiting outside. It would seem to have been unwise for Linda Fairstein, the assistant district attorney in charge of Manhattan sex crimes, to ignore, at the precinct house, the mother's assertion that the son was fifteen, and later to suggest, in court, that the boy's age had been unclear to her because the mother had used the word "minor."

It would also seem to have been unwise for Linda Fairstein to tell David Nocenti, the assistant U.S. Attorney who was paired with Yusef Salaam in a "Big Brother" program and who had come to the precinct house at the mother's request, that he had "no legal standing" there and that she would file a complaint with his supervisors. It would seem in this volatile a case imprudent of the police to follow their normal procedure by presenting Raymond Santana's initial statement in their own words, cop phrases that would predictably seem to some in the courtroom, as the expression of a fourteen-year-old held overnight and into the next afternoon for interrogation, unconvincing:

On April 19, 1989, at approximately 20:30 hours, I was at the Taft Projects in the vicinity of 113th St. and Madison Avenue. I was there with numerous friends. . . . At approximately 21:00 hours, we all (myself and approximately 15 others) walked south on Madison Avenue to E. 110th Street, then walked westbound to Fifth Avenue. At Fifth Avenue and 110th Street, we met up with an additional group of approximately 15 other males, who also entered Central Park with us at that location with the intent to rob cyclists and joggers . . .

In a case in which most of the defendants had made videotaped statements admitting at least some role in the assault and rape, this less than meticulous attitude toward the gathering and dissemination of information seemed peculiar and self-defeating, the kind of pressured or unthinking standard procedure that could not only exacerbate the fears and angers and suspicions of conspiracy shared by many blacks but open what seemed, on the basis of the confessions, a conclusive case to the kind of doubt that would eventually keep juries out, in the trial of the first three defendants, ten days, and, in the trial of the next two defendants, twelve days. One of the reasons the jury in the first trial could not agree, *Manhattan Lawyer* reported in its October 1990 issue, was that one juror, Ronald Gold, remained "deeply troubled by the discrepancies between the story [Antron] McCray tells on his videotaped statement and the prosecution's scenario":

Why did McCray place the rape at the reservoir, Gold demanded, when all evidence indicated it happened at the 102nd Street crossdrive? Why did McCray say the jog-ger was raped where she fell, when the prosecution said she'd been dragged 300 feet into the woods first? Why did McCray talk about having to hold her arms down, if she was found bound and gagged?

The debate raged for the last two days, with jurors dropping in and out of Gold's acquittal [for McCray] camp. . . .

After the jurors watched McCray's video for the fifth time, Miranda [Rafael Miranda, another juror] knew it well enough to cite the time-code numbers imprinted at the bottom of the videotape as her rebuffed Gold's argu-ments with specific statements from McCray's own lips. [McCray, on the videotape, after admitting that he had held the victim by her left arm as her clothes were pulled off, volunteered that he had "got on top" of her, and said that he had rubbed against her without an erection "so everybody would . . . just know I did it."] The pressure on Gold was mounting. Three jurors agree that it was evident Gold, worn down perhaps by his own displays of temper as much as anything else, capitulated out of exhaustion. While a bitter Gold told other jurors he felt terrible about ultimately giving in, Brueland [Harold Brueland, another juror who had for a time favored acquittal for McCray] believes it was all part of the process.

"I'd like to tell Ronnie someday that nervous exhaus-tion is an element built into the court system. They know that," Brueland says of court officials. "They know we're only going to be able to take it for so long. It's just a mat-ter of, you know, who's got the guts to stick with it."

So fixed were the emotions provoked by this case that the idea that there could have been, for even one juror, even a moment's doubt in the state's case, let alone the kind of doubt that could be sustained over ten days, seemed, to many in the city, bewildering, almost unthinkable: the attack on the jogger had by then passed into narrative, and the narrative was about confrontation, about what Governor Cuomo had called "the ultimate shriek of alarm," about what was wrong with the city and about its solution. What was wrong with the city had been identified, and its names were Raymond Santana, Yusef Salaam, Antron McCray, Kharey Wise, Kevin Richardson, and Steve Lopez. "They never could have thought of it as they raged through Central Park, tormenting and ruining people," Bob Herbert wrote in the *News* after the verdicts came in on the first three defendants.

There was no way it could have crossed their vicious minds. Running with the pack, they would have scoffed at the very idea. They would have laughed.

And yet it happened. In the end, Yusef Salaam, Antron McCray and Raymond Santana were nailed by a woman.

Elizabeth Lederer stood in the courtroom and watched Saturday night as the three were hauled off to jail. . . . At times during the trial, she looked about half the height of the long and lanky Salaam, who sneered at her from the witness stand. Salaam was apparently to dumb to realize that Lederer—this petite, soft-spoken, curly-haired prosecutor—was the jogger's avenger. . . .

You could tell that her thoughts were elsewhere, that she was thinking about the jogger.

You could tell that she was thinking: I did it.

I did it for you.

Do this in remembrance of me: the solution, then, or so such pervasive fantasies suggested, was to partake of the symbolic body and blood of The Jogger, whose idealization was by this point complete, and was rendered, significantly, in details stressing her "difference," or superior class. The Jogger was someone who wore, according to *Newsday,* "a light gold chain around her slender neck" as well as, according to the *News,* a "modest" gold ring and "a thin sheen" of lipstick. The Jogger was someone who would not, according to the *Post,* "even dignify her alleged attackers with a glance." The Jogger was someone who spoke, according to the *News,* in accents "suited to boardrooms," accents that might therefore seem "foreign to many native New Yorkers." In her first appearance on the witness stand she had been subjected, the *Times* noted, "to questions that most people do not have to answer publicly during their lifetimes," principally about her use of a diaphragm on the Sunday preceding the attack, and had answered these questions, according to an editorial in the *News,* with an "indomitable dignity" that had taught the city a lesson "about courage and class."

This emphasis on perceived refinements of character and of manner and of taste tended to distort and to flatten, and ultimately to suggest not the actual victim of an actual crime but a fictional character of a slightly earlier period, the well-brought-up virgin who briefly graces the city with her presence and receives in turn a taste of "real life." The defendants, by contrast, were seen as incapable of appreciating these marginal distinctions, ignorant of both the norms and accoutrements of middle-class life. "Did you have jogging clothes on?" Elizabeth Lederer asked Yusef Salaam, by way of trying to discredit his statement that he had gone into the park that night only to "walk around." Did he have "jogging clothes," did he have "sports equipment," did he have "a bicycle." A pernicious nostalgia had come to permeate the case, a longing for the New York that had seemed for a while to be about "sports equipment," about getting and spending rather than about having and not having: the reason that this victim must not be named was so that she could go unrecognized, it was astonishingly said, by Jerry Nachman, the editor of the *New York Post,* and then by others who seemed to find in this a particular resonance, to Bloomingdale's.

Some New York stories involving young middle-class white women do not make it to the editorial pages, or even necessarily to the front pages. In April 1990, a young middle-class white woman named Laurie Sue Rosenthal, raised in an Orthodox Jewish household and at age twenty-nine still living with her parents in Jamaica, Queens, happened to die, according to the coroner's report, from the accidental toxicity of Darvocet in combination with alcohol, in an apartment at 36 East 68th Street in Manhattan. The apartment belonged to the man she had been, according to her parents, seeing for about a year, a minor city assistant commissioner named Peter Franconeri. Peter Franconeri, who was at the time in charge of elevator and boiler inspections for the Building Department and married to someone else, wrapped Laurie Sue Rosenthal's body in a blanket; placed it, along with her handbag and ID, outside the building with the trash; and went to his office at 60 Hudson Street. At some point an anonymous call was made to 911. Franconeri was identified only after Laurie Sue Rosenthal's parents gave the police his beeper number, which they found in her address book. According to *Newsday,* which covered the story more extensively than the *News,* the *Post,* or the *Times,*

> Initial police reports indicated that there were no visible wounds on Rosenthal's body. But Rosenthal's mother, Ceil, said yesterday that the family was told the autopsy revealed two "unexplained bruises" on her daughter's body.
>
> Larry and Ceil Rosenthal said those findings seemed to support their suspicions that their daughter was upset because they received a call from their daughter at 3 A.M. Thursday "saying that he had beaten her up." The family reported the conversation to police.
>
> "I told her to get into a cab and get home," Larry Rosenthal said yesterday. "The next I heard was two detectives telling me terrible things."
>
> "The ME [medical examiner] said the bruises did not constitute a beating but they were going to examine them further," Ceil Rosenthal said.

"There were some minor bruises," a spokeswoman for the Office of the Chief Medical Examiner told *Newsday* a few days later, but the bruises "did not in any way contribute to her death." This is worth rerunning: A young woman calls her parents at three in the morning, "distraught." She says that she has been beaten up. A few hours later, on East 68th Street between Madison and Park avenues, a few steps from Porthault and Pratesi and Armani and Saint Laurent and the Westbury Hotel, at a time of day in this part of New York 10021 when Jim Buck's dog trainers are assembling their morning packs and Henry Kravis's Bentley is idling outside his Park Avenue apartment and the construction crews are clocking in over near the Frick at the multimillion-dollar houses under reconstruction for Bill Cosby and for the owner of The Limited, this young middle-class white woman's body, showing bruises, gets put out with the trash.

"Everybody got upside down because of who he was," an unidentified police officer later told Jim Dwyer of *Newsday,* referring to the man who put the young woman out with the trash. "If it had happened to anyone else, nothing would have come of it. A summons would have been issued and that would have been the end of it." In fact nothing did come of the death of Laurie Sue Rosenthal, which might have seemed a natural tabloid story but failed, on several levels, to catch the local imagination. For one thing she could not be trimmed into the role of the preferred tabloid victim, who is conventionally presented as fate's random choice (Laurie Sue Rosenthal had, for whatever reason, taken the Darvocet instead of a taxi home, her parents reported treatment for a previous Valium dependency, she could be presumed to have known over the course of a year that Franconeri was married and yet continued to see him); for another, she seemed not to have attended an expensive school or to have been employed in a glamour industry (no Ivy Grad, no Wall Street Exec), which made it hard to cast her as part of "what makes this city so vibrant and so great."

In August 1990, Peter Franconeri pled guilty to a misdemeanor, the unlawful removal of a body, and was sentenced by Criminal Court Judge Peter Benitez to seventy-five hours of community service. This was neither surprising nor much of a story (only twenty-three lines even in *Newsday,* on page twenty-nine of the city edition), and the case's lenient resolution was for many people a kind of relief. The district attorney's office had asked for "some incarceration," the amount usually described as a "touch," but no one wanted, it was said, to crucify the guy: Peter Franconeri was somebody who knew a lot of people, understood how to live in the city, who had for example not only the apartment on East 68th Street between Madison and Park but a house in Southampton and who also understood that putting a body outside with the trash was nothing to get upside down about, if it was handled right. Such understandings may in fact have been the city's true "ultimate shriek of alarm," but it was not a shriek the city wanted to recognize.

2

Perhaps the most arresting collateral news to surface, during the first few days after the attack on the Central Park jogger, was that a significant number of New Yorkers apparently believed the city sufficiently well-ordered to incorporate Central Park into their evening fitness schedules. "Prudence" was defined, even after the attack, as "staying south of 90th Street," or having "an awareness that you need to think about planning your routes," or, in the case of one woman interviewed by the *Times,* deciding to quit her daytime job (she was a lawyer) because she was "tired of being stuck out there, running later and later at night." "I don't think there's a runner who couldn't describe the silky, gliding feeling you get running at night," an editor of *Runner's World* told the *Times.* "You see less of what's around you and you become centered on your running."

The notion that Central Park at night might be a good place to "see less of what's around you" was recent. There were two reasons why Frederick Law Olmsted and Calvert Vaux, when they devised their winning entry in the 1858 competition for a Central Park design, decided to sink the transverse roads below grade level. One reason, the most often cited, was aesthetic, a recognition on the part of the designers that the four crossings specified by the terms of the competition, at 65th, 79th, 85th, and 97th streets, would intersect the sweep of the landscape, be "at variance with those agreeable sentiments which we should wish the park to inspire." The other reason, which appears to have been equally compelling, had to do with security. The problem with grade-level crossings, Olmsted and Vaux wrote in their "Greensward" plan, would be this:

> The transverse roads will . . . have to be kept open, while the park proper will be useless for any good purpose after

dusk; for experience has shown that even in London, with its admirable police arrangements, the public cannot be assured safe transit through large open spaces of ground after nightfall.

These public throughfares will then require to be well-lighted at the sides, and, to restrain marauders pursued by the police from escaping into the obscurity of the park, strong fences or walls, six or eight feet high, will be necessary.

The park, in other words, was seen from its conception as intrinsically dangerous after dark, a place of "obscurity," "useless for any good purpose," a refuge only for "marauders." The parks of Europe closed at nightfall, Olmsted noted in his 1882 pamphlet *The Spoils of the Park: With a Few Leaves from the Deep-laden Note-books of "A Wholly Unpractical Man,"* "but one surface road is kept open across Hyde Park, and the superintendent of the Metropolitan Police told me that a man's chances of being garrotted or robbed were, because of the facilities for concealment to be found in the Park, greater in passing at night along this road than anywhere else in London."

In the high pitch of the initial "jogger" coverage, suggesting as it did a city overtaken by animals, this pragmatic approach to urban living gave way to a more ideal construct, one in which New York either had once been or should be "safe," and now, as in Governor Cuomo's "none of us is safe," was not. It was time, accordingly, to "take it back," time to "say no"; time, as David Dinkins would put it during his campaign for the mayoralty in the summer of 1989, to "draw the line." What the line was to be drawn against was "crime," an abstract, a free-floating specter that could be dispelled by certain acts of personal affirmation, by the kind of moral rearmament that later figured in Mayor Dinkins's plan to revitalize the city by initiating weekly "Tuesday Night Out Against Crime" rallies.

By going into the park at night, Tom Wicker wrote in the *Times,* the victim in this case had "affirmed the primacy of freedom over fear." A week after the assault, Susan Chace suggested on the op-ed page of the *Times* that readers walk into the park at night and join hands. "A woman can't run in the park at an offbeat time," she wrote. "Accept it, you say. I can't. It shouldn't be like this in New York City, in 1989, in spring." Ronnie Eldridge also suggested that readers walk into the park at night, but to light candles. "Who are we that we allow ourselves to be chased out of the most magnificent part of our city?" she asked, and also: "If we give up the park, what are we supposed to do: fall back to Columbus Avenue and plant grass?" This was interesting, suggesting as it did that the city's not inconsiderable problems could be solved by the willingness of its citizens to hold or draw some line, to "say no"; in other words that a reliance on certain magical gestures could affect the city's fate.

The insistent sentimentalization of experience, which is to say the encouragement of such reliance, is not new in New York. A preference for broad strokes, for the distortion and flattening of character and the reduction of events to narrative, has been for well over a hundred years the heart of the way the city presents itself: Lady Liberty, huddled masses, ticker-tape parades, heroes, gutters, bright lights, broken hearts, eight million stories in the naked city; eight million stories and all the same story, each devised to obscure not only the city's actual tensions of race and class but also, more significantly, the civic and commercial arrangements that rendered those tensions irreconcilable.

Central Park itself was such a "story," an artificial pastoral in the nineteenth-century English romantic tradition, conceived, during a decade when the population of Manhattan would increase by 58 percent, as a civic project that would allow the letting of contracts and the employment of voters on a scale rarely before undertaken in New York. Ten million cartloads of dirt would need to be shifted during the twenty years of its construction. Four to five million trees and shrubs would need to be planted, half a million cubic yards of topsoil imported, 114 miles of ceramic pipe laid.

Nor need the completion of the park mean the end of the possibilities: in 1870, once William Marcy Tweed had revised the city charter and invented his Department of Public Parks, new roads could be built whenever jobs were needed. Trees could be dug up, and replanted. Crews could be set loose to prune, to clear, to hack at will. Frederick Law Olmsted, when he objected, could be overridden, and finally eased out. "A 'delegation' from a great political organization called on me by appointment," Olmsted wrote in *The Spoils of the Park,* recalling the conditions under which he had worked:

After introductions and handshakings, a circle was formed, and a gentleman stepped before me, and said, "We know how much pressed you must be . . . but at your convenience our association would like to have you determine what share of your patronage we can expect, and make suitable arrangements for our using it. We will take the liberty to suggest, sir, that there could be no more convenient way than that you should send us our due quota of tickets, if you will please, sir, in this form, *leaving us to fill in the name*." Here a packet of printed tickets was produced, from which I took one at random. It was a blank appointment and bore the signature of Mr. Tweed.

As superintendent of the Park, I once received in six days more than seven thousand letters of advice as to appointments, nearly all from men in office. . . . I have heard a candidate for a magisterial office in the city addressing from my doorsteps a crowd of such advice-bearers, telling them that I was bound to give them employment, and suggesting plainly, that, if I was slow about it, a rope round my neck might serve to lessen my reluctance to take good counsel. I have had a dozen men force their way into my house before I had risen from bed on a Sunday morning, and some break into my drawing room in their eagerness to deliver letters of advice.

Central Park, then, for its underwriters if not for Olmsted, was about contracts and concrete and kickbacks, about pork, but the sentimentalization that worked to obscure the pork, the "story," had to do with certain dramatic contrasts, or extremes, that were believed to characterize life in this as in no other city. These "contrasts," which have since become the very spine of the New York narrative, appeared early on: Philip Hone, the mayor of New York in 1826 and 1827, spoke in 1843 of a city "overwhelmed with population, and where the two extremes of costly luxury in living, expensive establishments and improvident wastes are presented in daily and hourly contrast with squalid mixing and hapless destruction." Given this narrative, Central Park could be and ultimately would be seen the way Olmsted himself saw it, as an essay in democracy, a social experiment meant to socialize a new immigrant population and to ameliorate the perilous separation of rich and poor. It was the duty and the interest of the city's privileged class, Olmsted had suggested some years before he designed Central Park, to "get up parks, gardens, music, dancing schools, reunions which will be so attractive as to force into contact the good and the bad, the gentleman and the rowdy."

The notion that the interests of the "gentleman" and the "rowdy" might be at odds did not intrude: then as now, the preferred narrative worked to veil actual conflict, to cloud the extent to which the condition of being rich was predicated upon the continued neediness of a working class; to confirm the responsible stewardship of "the gentleman" and to forestall the possibility of a self-conscious, or politicized, proletariat. Social and economic phenomena, in this narrative, were personalized. Politics were exclusively electoral. Problems were best addressed by the emergence and election of "leaders," who could in turn inspire the individual citizen to "participate," or "make a difference." "Will you help?" Mayor Dinkins asked New Yorkers, in a September 1990 address from St. Patrick's Cathedral intended as a response to the "New York crime wave" stories then leading the news. "Do you care? Are you ready to become part of the solution?"

"Stay," Governor Cuomo urged the same New Yorkers. "Believe. Participate. Don't give up." Manhattan borough president Ruth Messinger, at the dedication of a school flagpole, mentioned the importance of "getting involved" and "participating," or "pitching in to put the shine back on the Big Apple." In a discussion of the popular "New York" stories written between 1902 and 1910 by William Sidney Porter, or "O. Henry," William R. Taylor of the State University of New York at Stony Brook spoke of the way in which these stories, with their "focus on individuals' plights," their "absence of social or political implications" and "ideological neutrality," provided "a miraculous form of social glue":

These sentimental accounts of relations between classes in the city have a specific historical meaning: empathy without political compassion. They reduce the scale of human suffering to what atomized individuals endure as their plucky, sad lives were recounted week after week for almost a decade . . . their sentimental reading of oppression, class differences, human suffering, and affection helped create a new language for interpreting the city's complex society, a language that began to replace the threadbare moralism that New Yorkers inherited from 19th-century readings of the city. This language localized suffering in particular moments and confined it to par-

ticular occasions; it smoothed over differences because it
could be read almost the same way from either end of the
social scale.

Stories in which terrible crimes are inflicted on inno-
cent victims, offering as they do a similarly sentimental
reading of class differences and human suffering, a reading that promises both resolution and retribution, have
long performed as the city's endorphins, a built-in source
of natural morphine working to blur the edges of real
and to a great extent insoluble problems. What is singular
about New York, and remains virtually incomprehensible
to people who live in less rigidly organized parts of the
country, is the minimal level of comfort and opportunity
its citizens have come to accept. The romantic capitalist
pursuit of privacy and security and individual freedom, so
taken for granted nationally, plays, locally, not much role.
A city where virtually every impulse has been to stifle
rather than to encourage normal competition, New York
works, when it does work, not on a market economy
but on little deals, payoffs, accommodations, baksheesh,
arrangements that circumvent the direct exchange of
goods and services and prevent what would be, in a competitive economy, the normal ascendance of the superior
product.

There were in the five boroughs in 1990 only 581
supermarkets (a supermarket, as defined by the trade
magazine *Progressive Grocer,* is a market that does an annual
volume of $2 million), or, assuming a population of eight
million, one supermarket for every 13,769 citizens. Gro-
ceries, costing more than they should because of this

absence of competition and also because of the proliferation of payoffs required to ensure this absence of competition (produce, we have come to understand, belongs to the Gambinos, and fish to the Lucheses and the Genoveses, and a piece of the construction of the market to each of the above, but keeping the door open belongs finally to the inspector here, the inspector there), are carried home or delivered, as if in Jakarta, by pushcart.

It has historically taken, in New York as if in Mexico City, ten years to process and specify and bid and contract and construct a new school; twenty or thirty years to build or, in the cases of Bruckner Boulevard and the West Side Highway, to not quite build a highway. A recent public scandal revealed that a batch of city-ordered Pap smears had gone unread for more than a year (in the developed world the Pap smear, a test for cervical cancer, is commonly read within a few days); what did not become a public scandal, what is still accepted as the way things are, is that even Pap smears ordered by Park Avenue gynecologists can go unread for several weeks.

Such resemblances to cities of the third world are in no way casual, or based on the "color" of a polyglot population: these are all cities arranged primarily not to improve the lives of their citizens but to be labor-intensive, to accommodate, ideally at the subsistence level, since it is at the subsistence level that the work force is most apt to be captive and loyalty assured, a third-world population. In some ways New York's very attractiveness, its promises of opportunity and improved wages, its commitments as a city in the developed world, were what seemed destined to render it ultimately unworkable. Where the vitality of such cities in the less developed world had depended on their ability to guarantee low-cost labor and an absence of regulation, New York had historically depended instead on the constant welling up of new businesses, of new employers to replace those phased out, like the New York garment manufacturers who found it cheaper to make their clothes in Hong Kong or Kuala Lumpur or Taipei, by rising local costs.

It had been the old pattern of New York, supported by an expanding national economy, to lose one kind of business and gain another. It was the more recent error of New York to misconstrue this history of turnover as an indestructible resource, there to be taxed at will, there to be regulated whenever a dollar could be seen in doing so, there for the taking. By 1977, New York had lost some 600,000 jobs, most of them in manufacturing and in the kinds of small businesses that could no longer maintain their narrow profit margins inside the city. During the "recovery" years, from 1977 until 1988, most of these jobs were indeed replaced, but in a potentially perilous way: of the 500,000 new jobs created, most were in the area most vulnerable to a downturn, that of financial and business services, and many of the rest in an area not only equally vulnerable to bad times but dispiriting to the city even in good, that of tourist and restaurant services.

The demonstration that many kinds of businesses were finding New York expendable had failed to prompt real efforts to make the city more competitive. Taxes grew still more punitive, regulation more Byzantine. Forty-nine thousand new jobs were created in New York's city agencies between 1983 and 1990, even as the services provided by those agencies were widely perceived to decline. Attempts at "reform" typically tended to create more jobs: in 1988, in response to the length of time it was taking to build or repair a school, a new agency, the School Construction Authority, was formed. A New York City school, it was said, would now take only five years to build. The head of the School Construction Authority was to receive $145,000 a year and each of the three vice presidents $110,000 a year. An executive gym, with Nautilus equipment, was contemplated for the top floor of the agency's new headquarters at the International Design Center in Long Island City. Two years into this reform, the backlog on repairs to existing schools stood at thirty-three thousand outstanding requests. "To relieve the charity of friends of the support of a half-blind and half-witted man by employing him at the public expense as an inspector of cement may not be practical with reference to the permanent firmness of a wall," Olmsted noted after his Central Park experience, "while it is perfectly so with reference to the triumph of sound doctrine at an election."

In fact the highest per capita taxes of any city in the United States (and, as anyone running a small business knows, the widest variety of taxes) provide, in New York, unless the citizen is prepared to cut a side deal here and there, only the continuing multiplication of regulations designed to benefit the contractors and agencies and unions with whom the regulators have cut their own deals. A kitchen appliance accepted throughout the rest of the United States as a basic postwar amenity, the in-sink garbage disposal unit, is for example illegal in New York.

Disposals, a city employee advised me, not only encourage rats, and "bacteria," presumably in a way that bags of garbage sitting on the sidewalk do not ("Because it is," I was told when I asked how this could be), but also encourage people "to put their babies down them."

On the one hand this illustrates how a familiar urban principle, that of patronage (the more garbage there is to be collected, the more garbage collectors can be employed), can be reduced, in the bureaucratic wilderness that is any third-world city, to voodoo; on the other it reflects this particular city's underlying criminal ethic, its acceptance of graft and grift as the bedrock of every transaction. "Garbage costs are outrageous," an executive of Supermarkets General, which owns Pathmark, recently told *City Limits* about why the chains preferred to locate in the suburbs. "Every time you need to hire a contractor, it's a problem." The problem, however, is one from which not only the contractor but everyone with whom the contractor does business—a chain of direct or indirect patronage extending deep into the fabric of the city—stands to derive one or another benefit, which was one reason the death of a young middle-class white woman in the East 68th Street apartment of the assistant commissioner in charge of boiler and elevator inspections flickered so feebly on the local attention span.

It was only within the transforming narrative of "contrasts" that both the essential criminality of the city and its related absence of civility could become points of pride, evidence of "energy": if you could make it here you could make it anywhere, hello sucker, get smart. Those who did not get the deal, who bought retail, who did not know what it took to get their electrical work signed off, were dismissed as provincials, bridge-and-tunnels, out-of-towners who did not have what it took not to get taken. "Every tourist's nightmare became a reality for a Maryland couple over the weekend when the husband was beaten and robbed on Fifth Avenue in front of Trump Tower," began a story in the *New York Post* during the summer of 1990. "Where do you think we're from, Iowa?" the prosecutor who took Robert Chambers's statement said on videotape by way of indicating that he doubted Chambers's version of Jennifer Levin's death. "They go after poor people like you from out of town, they prey on the tourists," a clerk explained in the West 46th Street computer store where my husband and I had taken refuge to escape three muggers. My husband said that we lived in New York. "That's why they didn't get you," the clerk said, effortlessly incorporating this change in the data. "That's how you could move fast."

The narrative comforts us, in other words, with the assurance that the world is knowable, even flat, and New York its center, its motor, its dangerous but vital "energy." "Family in Fatal Mugging Loved New York" was the *Times* headline on a story following the September 1990 murder, in the Seventh Avenue IND station, of a twenty-two-year-old tourist from Utah. The young man, his parents, his brother, and his sister-in-law had attended the U.S. Open and were reportedly on their way to dinner at a Moroccan restaurant downtown. "New York, to them, was the greatest place in the world," a family friend from Utah was quoted as having said. Since the narrative requires that the rest of the country provide a dramatic contrast to New York, the family's hometown in Utah was characterized by the *Times* as a place where "life revolves around the orderly rhythms of Brigham Young University" and "there is only about one murder a year." The town was in fact Provo, where Gary Gilmore shot the hotel manager, both in life and in *The Executioner's Song.* "She loved New York, she just loved it," a friend of the assaulted jogger told the *Times* after the attack. "I think she liked the fast pace, the competitiveness."

New York, the *Times* concluded, "invigorated" the jogger, "matched her energy level." At a time when the city lay virtually inert, when forty thousand jobs had been wiped out in the financial markets and former traders were selling shirts at Bergdorf Goodman for Men, when the rate of mortgage delinquencies had doubled, when fifty or sixty million square feet of office space remained unrented (sixty million square feet of unrented office space is the equivalent of fifteen darkened World Trade Towers) and even prime commercial blocks on Madison Avenue in the Seventies were boarded up, empty; at a time when the money had dropped out of all the markets and the Europeans who had lent the city their élan and their capital during the eighties had moved on, vanished to more cheerful venues, this notion of the city's "energy" was sedative, as was the commandeering of "crime" as the city's central problem.

3

The extent to which the October 1987 crash of the New York financial markets damaged the illusions of infinite recovery and growth on which the city had operated during the 1980s had been at first hard to apprehend. "Ours is a time of New York ascendant," the New York City Commission of the Year 2000, created during the mayoralty of Edward Koch to reflect the best thinking of the city's various business and institutional establishments, had declared in its 1987 report. "The city's economy is stronger than it has been in decades, and is driven both by its own resilience and by the national economy; New York is more than ever the international capital of finance, and the gateway to the American economy."

And then, its citizens had come gradually to understand, it was not. This perception that something was "wrong" in New York had been insidious, a slow-onset illness at first noticeable only in periods of temporary remission. Losses that might have seemed someone else's problem (or even comeuppance) as the markets were in their initial 1987 free-fall, and that might have seemed more remote still as the markets regained the appearance of strength, had come imperceptibly but inexorably to alter the tone of daily life. By April of 1990, people who lived in and around New York were expressing, in interviews with the *Times,* considerable anguish and fear that they did so: "I feel very resentful that I've lost a lot of flexibility in my life," one said. "I often wonder, 'Am I crazy for coming here?'" "People feel a sense of impending doom about what may happen to them," a clinical psychologist said. People were "frustrated," "feeling absolutely desolate," "trapped," "angry," "terrified," and "on the verge of panic."

It was a panic that seemed in many ways specific to New York, and inexplicable outside it. Even later, when the troubles of New York had become a common theme, Americans from less depressed venues had difficulty comprehending the nature of those troubles, and tended to attribute them, as New Yorkers themselves had come to do, to "crime." "Escape From New York" was the headline on the front page of the *New York Post* on September 10, 1990. "Rampaging Crime Wave Has 59% of Residents Terrified. Most Would Get Out of the City, Says Time/CNN Poll." This poll appeared in the edition of *Time* dated September 17, 1990, which carried the cover legend "The Rotting of the Big Apple." "Reason: a surge of drugs and violent crime that government officials seem utterly unable to combat," the story inside explained. Columnists referred, locally, to "this sewer of a city." The *Times* ran a plaintive piece about the snatch of Elizabeth Rohatyn's Hermès handbag outside Arcadia, a restaurant on East 62nd Street that had for a while seemed the very heart of the New York everyone now missed, the New York where getting and spending could take place without undue reference to having and not having, the duty-free New York; that this had occurred to the wife of Felix Rohatyn, who was widely perceived to have saved the city from its fiscal crisis in the midseventies, seemed to many a clarion irony.

This question of crime was tricky. There were in fact

eight American cities with higher homicide rates, and twelve with higher overall crime rates. Crime had long been taken for granted in the less affluent parts of the city, and had become in the midseventies, as both unemployment and the costs of maintaining property rose and what had once been functioning neighborhoods were abandoned and burned and left to whomever claimed them, endemic. "In some poor neighborhoods, crime became almost a way of life," Jim Sleeper, an editor at *Newsday* and the author of *The Closest of Strangers: Liberalism and the Politics of Race in New York,* noted in his discussion of the social disintegration that occurred during this period:

> . . . a subculture of violence with complex bonds of utility and affection within families and the larger, "law-abiding" community. Struggling merchants might "fence" stolen goods, for example, thus providing quick cover and additional incentive for burglaries and robberies; the drug economy became more vigorous, reshaping criminal lifestyles and tormenting the loyalties of families and friends. A walk down even a reasonably busy street in a poor, minority neighborhood at high noon could become an unnerving journey into a landscape eerie and grim.

What seemed markedly different a decade later, what made crime a "story," was that the more privileged, and especially the more privileged white, citizens of New York had begun to feel unnerved at high noon in even their own neighborhoods. Although New York City Police Department statistics suggested that white New Yorkers were not actually in increased mortal danger (the increase in homicides between 1977 and 1989, from 1,557 to 1,903, was entirely among what the NYPD classified as Hispanic, Asian, and black victims; the number of white murder victims had steadily declined, from 361 in 1977 to 227 in 1984 and 190 in 1989), the apprehension of such danger, exacerbated by street snatches and muggings and the quite useful sense that the youth in the hooded sweatshirt with his hands jammed in his pockets might well be a predator, had become general. These more privileged New Yorkers now felt unnerved not only on the street, where the necessity for evasive strategies had become an exhausting constant, but in even the most insulated and protected apartment buildings. As the residents of such buildings, the owners of twelve- and sixteen- and twenty-four-room apartments, watched the potted ficus trees disappear from outside their doors and the graffiti appear on their limestone walls and the smashed safety glass from car windows get swept off their sidewalks, it had become increasingly easy to imagine the outcome of a confrontation between, say, the relief night doorman and six dropouts from Julia Richman High School on East 67th Street.

And yet those New Yorkers who had spoken to the *Times* in April of 1990 about their loss of flexibility, about their panic, their desolation, their anger, and their sense of impending doom, had not been talking about drugs, or crime, or any of the city's more publicized and to some extent inflated ills. These were people who did not for the most part have twelve- and sixteen-room apartments and doormen and the luxury of projected fears. These people were talking instead about an immediate fear, about money, about the vertiginous plunge in the value of their houses and apartments and condominiums, about the possibility or probability of foreclosure and loss; about, implicitly, their fears of being left, like so many they saw every day, below the line, out in the cold, on the street.

This was a climate in which many of the questions that had seized the city's attention in 1987 and 1988, for example that of whether Mortimer Zuckerman should be "allowed" to build two fifty-nine-story office towers on the site of what is now the Coliseum, seemed in retrospect wistful, the baroque concerns of better times. "There's no way anyone would make a sane judgment to go into the ground now," a vice president at Cushman and Wakefield told the *New York Observer* about the delay in the Coliseum project, which had in fact lost its projected major tenant, Salomon Brothers, shortly after Black Monday, 1987. "It would be suicide. You're better off sitting in a tub of water and opening your wrists." Such fears were, for a number of reasons, less easy to incorporate into the narrative than the fear of crime.

The imposition of a sentimental, or false, narrative on the disparate and often random experience that constitutes the life of a city or a country means, necessarily, that much of what happens in that city or country will be rendered merely illustrative, a series of set pieces, or performance opportunities. Mayor Dinkins could, in such a symbolic substitute for civic life, "break the boycott" (the Flatbush boycott organized to mobilize resentment of

Korean merchants in black neighborhoods) by purchasing a few dollars' worth of produce from a Korean grocer on Church Avenue. Governor Cuomo could "declare war on crime" by calling for five thousand additional police; Mayor Dinkins could "up the ante" by calling for sixty-five hundred. "White slut comes into the park looking for the African man," a black woman could say, her voice loud but still conversational, in the corridor outside the courtroom where, during the summer of 1990, the first three defendants in the Central Park attack, Antron McCray, Yusef Salaam, and Raymond Santana, were tried on charges of attempted murder, assault, sodomy, and rape. "Boyfriend beats shit out of her, they blame it on our boys," the woman could continue, and then, refer- ring to a young man with whom the victim had at one time split the cost of an apartment: "How about the roommate, anybody test his semen? No. He's white. They don't do it to each other."

Glances could then flicker among those reporters and producers and courtroom sketch artists and photogra- phers and cameramen and techs and summer interns who assembled daily at 111 Centre Street. Cellular phones could be picked up, a show of indifference. Small talk could be exchanged with the marshals, a show of solidar- ity. The woman could then raise her voice: "White folk, all of them are devils, even those that haven't been born yet, they are *devils*. Little *demons*. I don't understand these devils, I guess they think this is *their court.*" The reporters could gaze beyond her, faces blank, no eye contact, a more correct form of hostility and also more lethal. The woman could hold her ground but avert her eyes, letting her gaze fall on another black, in this instance a black *Daily News* columnist, Bob Herbert. "You," she could say. "You are a *disgrace*. Go ahead. Line up there. Line up with the white folk. Look at them, lining up for their first-class seats while *my* people are downstairs behind *barricades* . . . kept behind barricades like *cattle* . . . not even allowed in the room to see their sons lynched . . . is that an *African* I see in that line? Or is that a *Negro.* Oh, oh, sorry, shush, white folk didn't know, he was *passing . . .*"

In a city in which grave and disrupting problems had become general—problems of not having, problems of not making it, problems that demonstrably existed, among the mad and the ill and the underequipped and the overwhelmed, with decreasing reference to color—the case of the Central Park jogger provided more than just a safe, or structured, setting in which various and some-times only marginally related rages could be vented. "This trial," the *Daily News* announced on its editorial page one morning in July 1990, midway through the trial of the first three defendants, "is about more than the rape and the brutalization of a single woman. It is about the rape and the brutalization of a city. The jogger is a symbol of all that's wrong here. And all that's right, because she is nothing less than an inspiration."

The *News* did not define the ways in which "the rape and the brutalization of the city" manifested itself, nor was definition necessary: this was a city in which the threat or the fear of brutalization had become so imme-diate that citizens were urged to take up their own defense, to form citizen patrols or militia, as in Beirut. This was a city in which between twenty and thirty neighborhoods had already given over their protection, which was to say the right to determine who belonged in the neighborhood and who did not and what should be done about it, to the Guardian Angels. This was a city in which a Brooklyn vigilante group, which called itself Crack Busters and was said to be trying to rid its Bedford-Stuyvesant neighborhood of drugs, would before September was out "settle an argument" by dousing with gasoline and setting on fire an abandoned van and the three homeless citizens inside. This was a city in which the *Times* would soon perceive, in the failing economy, "a bright side for the city at large," the bright side being that while there was believed to have been an increase in the number of middle-income and upper-income families who wanted to leave the city, "the slumping market is keeping many of those families in New York."

In this city rapidly vanishing into the chasm between its actual life and its preferred narratives, what people said when they talked about the case of the Central Park jogger came to seem a kind of poetry, a way of expressing, without directly stating, different but equally volatile and similarly occult visions of the same disaster. One vision, shared by those who had seized upon the attack on the jogger as an exact representation of what was wrong with the city, was of a city systematically ruined, violated, raped by its underclass. The opposing vision, shared by those who had seized upon the arrest of the defendants as an exact representation of their own victimization, was of a city in which the powerless had been systematically ruined, violated, raped by the powerful. For so long as this case held the city's febrile attention, then, it offered a narrative for the city's distress, a frame in which the actual social and economic forces wrenching the city could be personalized and ultimately obscured.

Or rather it offered two narratives, mutually exclusive. Among a number of blacks, particularly those whose experience with or distrust of the criminal justice system was such that they tended to discount the fact that five of the six defendants had to varying degrees admitted taking part in the attack, and to focus instead on the absence of any supporting forensic evidence incontrovertibly linking this victim to these defendants, the case could be read as a confirmation not only of their victimization but of the white conspiracy they saw at the heart of that victimization. For the *Amsterdam News,* which did not veer automatically to the radical analysis (a typical issue in the fall of 1990 lauded the FBI for its minority recruiting and the Harlem National Guard for its high morale and readiness to go to the Gulf), the defendants could in this light be seen as victims of "a political trial," of a "legal lynching," of a case "rigged from the very beginning" by the decision of "the white press" that "whoever was arrested and charged in this case of the attempted murder, rape, and sodomy of a well-connected, bright, beautiful, and promising white woman was guilty, pure and simple."

For Alton H. Maddox, Jr., the message to be drawn from the case was that the American criminal justice system, which was under any circumstances "inherently and unabashedly racist," failed "to function equitably at any level when a Black male is accused of raping a white female." For others the message was more general, and worked to reinforce the fragile but functional mythology

of a heroic black past, the narrative in which European
domination could be explained as a direct and vengeful
response to African superiority. "Today the white man is
faced head-on with what is happening on the Black Continent, Africa," Malcolm X wrote.

> Look at the artifacts being discovered there, that are
> proving over and over again, how the black man had
> great, fine, sensitive civilizations before the white man
> was out of the caves. Below the Sahara, in the places
> where most of America's Negroes' foreparents were kid-
> napped, there is being unearthed some of the finest
> craftsmanship, sculpture and other objects, that has ever
> been seen by modern man. Some of these things now are
> on view in such places as New York City's Museum of
> Modern Art. Gold work of such fine tolerance and work-
> manship that it has no rival. Ancient objects produced by
> black hands . . . refined by those black hands with results
> that no human hand today can equal.
>
> History has been so "whitened" by the white man that
> even the black professors have known little more than the
> most ignorant black man about the talents and rich civi-
> lizations and cultures of the black man of millenniums
> ago . . .

"Our proud African queen," the Reverend Al Sharpton
had said of Tawana Brawley's mother, Glenda Brawley:
"She stepped out of anonymity, stepped out of obscurity,
and walked into history." It was said in the corridors of
the courthouse where Yusuf Salaam was tried that he carried himself "like an African king."

"It makes no difference anymore whether the attack on Tawana happened," William Kunstler had told *New York Newsday* when the alleged rape and torture of Tawana Brawley by a varying number of white police officers seemed, as an actual prosecutable crime if not as a window on what people needed to believe, to have dematerialized. "If her story was a concoction to prevent her parents from punishing her for staying out all night, that doesn't disguise the fact that a lot of young black women are treated the way she said she was treated." The importance of whether or not the crime had occurred was, in this view, entirely resident in the crime's "description," which was defined by Stanley Diamond in *The Nation* as "a crime that did not occur" but was "described with skill and controlled hysteria by the black actors as the epitome of degradation, a repellent model of what actually happens to too many black women."

A good deal of what got said around the edges of the jogger case, in the corridors and on the call-in shows, seemed to derive exclusively from the suspicions of conspiracy increasingly entrenched among those who believe themselves powerless. A poll conducted in June of 1990 by the *New York Times* and WCBS-TV News determined that 77 percent of blacks polled believed either that it was "true" or "might possibly be true" (as opposed to "almost certainly not true") that the government of the United States "singles out and investigates black elected officials in order to discredit them in a way it doesn't do with white officials." Sixty percent believed that it was true or might possibly be true that the government "deliberately makes sure that drugs are easily available in poor black neighborhoods in order to harm black people." Twenty-nine percent believed that it was true or might possibly be true that "the virus that causes AIDS was deliberately created in a laboratory in order to infect black people." In each case, the alternative response to "true" or "might possibly be true" was "almost certainly not true," which might have seemed in itself to reflect a less than ringing belief in the absence of conspiracy. "The conspiracy to destroy Black boys is very complex and interwoven," Jawanza Kunjufu, a Chicago educational consultant, wrote in his *Countering the Conspiracy to Destroy Black Boys,* a 1982 pamphlet that has since been extended to three volumes.

> There are many contributors to the conspiracy, ranging from the very visible who are more obvious, to the less visible and silent partners who are more difficult to recognize.
>
> Those people who adhere to the doctrine of white racism, imperialism, and white male supremacy are easier to recognize. Those people who actively promote drugs and gang violence are active conspirators, and easier to identify. What makes the conspiracy more complex are those people who do not plot together to destroy Black boys, but, through their indifference, perpetuate it. This passive group of conspirators consists of parents, educators, and white liberals who deny being racists, but through their silence allow institutional racism to continue.

For those who proceeded from the conviction that there was under way a conspiracy to destroy blacks, particularly black boys, a belief in the innocence of these defendants, a conviction that even their own statements had been rigged against them or wrenched from them, followed logically. It was in the corridors and on the call-in shows that the conspiracy got sketched in, in a series of fantasy details that conflicted not only with known facts but even with each other. It was said that the prosecution was withholding evidence that the victim had gone to the park to meet a drug dealer. It was said, alternately or concurrently, that the prosecution was withholding evidence that the victim had gone to the park to take part in a satanic ritual. It was said that the forensic photographs showing her battered body were not "real" photographs, that "they," the prosecution, had "brought in some corpse for the pictures." It was said that the young woman who appeared on the witness stand and identified herself as the victim was not the "real" victim, that "they" had in this case brought in an actress.

What was being expressed in each instance was the sense that secrets must be in play, that "they," the people who had power in the courtroom, were in possession of information systematically withheld—since information itself was power—from those who did not have power. On the day the first three defendants were sentenced, C. Vernon Mason, who had formally entered the case in the penalty phase as Antron McCray's attorney, filed a brief that included the bewildering and untrue assertion that the victim's boyfriend, who had not at that time been called to testify, was black. That some whites jumped to engage this assertion on its own terms (the *Daily News* columnist Gail Collins referred to it as Mason's "slimiest argument of the hour—an announcement that the jogger had a black lover") tended only to reinforce the sense of racial estrangement that was the intended subtext of the assertion, which was without meaning or significance except in that emotional deep where whites are seen as conspiring in secret to sink blacks in misery. "Just answer me, who got addicted?" I recall one black spectator asking another as they left the courtroom. "I'll tell you who got addicted, the inner city got addicted." He had with him a pamphlet that laid out a scenario in which the government had conspired to exterminate blacks by flooding their neighborhoods with drugs, a scenario touching all the familiar points, Laos, Cambodia, the Golden Triangle, the CIA, more secrets, more poetry.

"From the beginning I have insisted that this was not a racial case," Robert Morgenthau, the Manhattan district attorney, said after the verdicts came in on the first jogger trial. He spoke of those who, in his view, wanted "to divide the races and advance their own private agendas," and of how the city was "ill-served" by those who had so "sought to exploit" this case. "We had hoped that the racial tensions surrounding the jogger trial would begin to dissipate soon after the jury arrived at a verdict," a *Post* editorial began a few days later. The editorial spoke of an "ugly claque of 'activists,'" of the "divisive atmosphere" they had created, and of the anticipation with which the city's citizens had waited for "mainstream black leaders" to step forward with praise for the way in which the verdicts had brought New York "back from the brink of criminal chaos":

> Alas, in the jogger case, the wait was in vain. Instead of praise for a verdict which demonstrated that sometimes criminals are caught and punished, New Yorkers heard charlatans like the Rev. Al Sharpton claim the case was fixed. They heard that C. Vernon Mason, one of the engineers of the Tawana Brawley hoax—the attorney who thinks Mayor Dinkins wears "too many yarmulkes"— was planning to appeal the verdicts . . .

To those whose preferred view of the city was of an inherently dynamic and productive community ordered by the natural play of its conflicting elements, enriched, as in Mayor Dinkins's "gorgeous mosaic," by its very "contrasts," this case offered a number of useful elements. There was the confirmation of "crime" as the canker corroding the life of the city. There was, in the random and feral evening described by the East Harlem attackers and the clear innocence of and damage done to the Upper East Side and Wall Street victim, an eerily exact and conveniently personalized representation of what the *Daily News* had called "the rape and the brutalization of a city." Among the reporters on this case, whose own narrative conventions involved "hero cops" and "brave prosecutors" going hand to hand against "crime" (the "Secret Agony of Jogger DA," we learned in the *Post* a few days after the verdicts in the first trial, was that "Brave Prosecutor's Marriage Failed as She Put Rapists Away"), there seemed an unflagging enthusiasm for the repetition and reinforcement of these elements, and an equally unflagging resistance, even hostility, to exploring the point of view of the defendants' families and friends and personal or political allies (or, as they were called in news reports, the "supporters") who gathered daily at the other end of the corridor from the courtroom.

This seemed curious. Criminal cases are widely regarded by American reporters as windows on the city or culture in which they take place, opportunities to enter not only households but parts of the culture normally closed, and yet this was a case in which indifference to the world of the defendants extended even to the reporting of names and occupations. Yusuf Salaam's mother, who happened to be young and photogenic and to have European features, was pictured so regularly that she and her son became the instantly recognizable "images" of Jogger One, but even then no one got her name quite right. For a while in the papers she was "Cheroney," or sometimes "Cheronay," McEllhonor, then she became Cheroney McEllhonor Salaam. After she testified, the spelling of her first name was corrected to "Sharonne," although, since the byline on a piece she wrote for the *Amsterdam News* spelled it differently, "Sharrone," this may have been another misunderstanding. Her occupation was frequently given as "designer" (later, after her son's conviction, she went to work as a paralegal for William Kunstler), but no one seemed to take this seriously enough to say what she designed or for whom; not until after she testified, when *Newsday* reported her testimony that on the evening of her son's arrest she had arrived at the precinct house late because she was an instructor at the Parsons School of Design, did the notion of "designer" seem sufficiently concrete to suggest an actual occupation.

The Jogger One defendants were referred to repeatedly in the news columns of the *Post* as "thugs." The defendants and their families were often said by reporters to be "sneering." (The reporters, in turn, were said at the other end of the corridor to be "smirking.") "We don't have nearly so strong a question as to the guilt or innocence of the defendants as we did at Bensonhurst," a *Newsday* reporter covering the first jogger trial said to the *New York Observer*, well before the closing arguments, by way of explaining why *Newsday*'s coverage may have seemed less extensive on this trial than on the Bensonhurst trials. "There is not a big question as to what happened in Central Park that night. Some details are missing, but it's fairly clear who did what to whom."

In fact this came close to the heart of it: that it seemed, on the basis of the videotaped statements, fairly clear who had done what to whom was precisely the case's liberating aspect, the circumstance that enabled many of the city's citizens to say and think what they might otherwise have left unexpressed. Unlike other recent high-visibility cases in New York, unlike Bensonhurst and unlike Howard Beach and unlike Bernhard Goetz, here was a case in which the issue not exactly of race but of an increasingly visible underclass could be confronted by the middle class, both white and black, without guilt. Here was a case that gave this middle class a way to transfer and express what had clearly become a growing and previously inadmissible rage with the city's disorder, with the entire range of ills and uneasy guilts that came to mind in a city where entire families slept in the discarded boxes in which new Sub-Zero refrigerators were delivered, at twenty-six hundred per, to more affluent families. Here was also a case, most significantly, in which even that transferred rage could be transferred still further, veiled, personalized: a case in which the city's distress could be seen to derive not precisely from its underclass but instead from certain identifiable individuals who claimed to speak for this underclass, individuals who, in Robert Morganthau's words, "sought to exploit" this case, to "advance their own private agendas"; individuals who wished even to "divide the races."

If the city's problems could be seen as deliberate disruptions of a naturally cohesive and harmonious community, a community in which, undisrupted, "contrasts" generated a perhaps dangerous but vital "energy," then those problems were tractable, and could be addressed, like "crime," by the call for "better leadership." Considerable comfort could be obtained, given this story line, through the demonization of the Reverend Al Sharpton, whose presence on the edges of certain criminal cases that interested him had a polarizing effect that tended to reinforce the narrative. Jim Sleeper, in *The Closest of Strangers,* described one of the fifteen marches Sharpton led through Bensonhurst after the 1989 killing of an East New York sixteen-year-old, Yusuf Hawkins, who had come into Bensonhurst and been set upon, with baseball bats and ultimately with bullets, by a group of young whites.

An August 27, 1989, *Daily News* photo of the Reverend Al Sharpton and a claque of black teenagers marching in Bensonhurst to protest Hawkins's death shows that they are not really "marching." They are stumbling along, huddled together, heads bowed under the storm of hatred breaking over them, eyes wide, hanging on to one another and to Sharpton, scared out of their wits. They, too, are innocents—or were until that day, which they will always remember. And because Sharpton is with them, his head bowed, his face showing that he knows what they're feeling, he is in the hearts of black people all over New York.

Yet something is wrong with this picture. Sharpton did not invite or coordinate with Bensonhurst community leaders who wanted to join the march. Without the time for organizing which these leaders should have been given in order to rein in the punks who stood waving watermelons; without an effort by black leaders more reputable than Sharpton to recruit whites citywide and swell the march, Sharpton was assured that the punks would carry the day. At several points he even baited them by blowing kisses . . .

"I knew that Bensonhurst would clarify whether it had been a racial incident or not," Sharpton said by way of explaining, on a recent *Frontline* documentary, his strategy in Bensonhurst. "The fact that I was so controversial to Bensonhurst helped them forget that the cameras were there," he said. "So I decided to help them. . . . I would throw kisses to them, and they would go nuts." *Question,* began a joke told in the aftermath of the first jogger trial. *You're in a room with Hitler, Saddam Hussein, and Al Sharpton. You have only two bullets. Who do you shoot? Answer: Al Sharpton. Twice.*

Sharpton did not exactly fit the roles New York traditionally assigns, for maximum audience comfort, to prominent blacks. He seemed in many ways a phantasm, somebody whose instinct for the connections between religion and politics and show business was so innate that he had been all his life the vessel for other people's hopes and fears. He had given his first sermon at age four. He was touring with Mahalia Jackson at eleven. As a teenager, according to Robert D. McFadden, Ralph Blumenthal, M. A. Farber, E. R. Shipp, Charles Strum, and Craig Wolff, the *New York Times* reporters and editors who collaborated on *Outrage: The Story Behind the Tawana Brawley Hoax,* Sharpton was tutored first by Adam Clayton Powell, Jr. ("You got to know when to hit it and you got to know when to quit it and when it's quittin' time, don't push it," Powell told him), then by the Reverend Jesse Jackson ("Once you turn on the gas, you got to cook or burn 'em up," Jackson told him), and eventually, after obtaining a grant from Bayard Rustin and campaigning for Shirley Chisholm, by James Brown. "Once, he trailed Brown down a corridor, through a door, and, to his astonishment, onto a stage flooded with spotlights," the authors of *Outrage* reported. "He immediately went into a wiggle and dance."

It was perhaps this talent for seizing the spotlight and the moment, this fatal bent for the wiggle and the dance, that most clearly disqualified Sharpton from casting as the

Good Negro, the credit to the race, the exemplary if often imagined figure whose refined manners and good grammar could be stressed and who could be seen to lay, as Jimmy Walker said of Joe Louis, "a rose on the grave of Abraham Lincoln." It was left, then, to cast Sharpton, and for Sharpton to cast himself, as the Outrageous Nigger, the familiar role—assigned sixty years ago to Father Divine and thirty years later to Adam Clayton Powell—of the essentially manageable fraud whose first concern is his own well-being. It was, for example, repeatedly mentioned, during the ten days the jury was out on the first jogger trial, that Sharpton had chosen to wait out the verdict not at 111 Centre Street but "in the air-conditioned comfort" of C. Vernon Mason's office, from which he could be summoned by beeper.

Sharpton, it was frequently said by whites and also by some blacks, "represented nobody," was "self-appointed" and "self-promoting." He was an "exploiter" of blacks, someone who "did them more harm than good." It was pointed out that he had been indicted by the state of New York in June of 1989 on charges of grand larceny. (He was ultimately acquitted.) It was pointed out that *New York Newsday,* working on information that appeared to have been supplied by federal law-enforcement agencies, had in January 1988 named him as a federal informant, and that he himself admitted to having let the government tap his phone in a drug-enforcement effort. It was routinely said, most tellingly of all in a narrative based on the magical ability of "leaders" to improve the commonweal, that he was "not the right leader," "not at all the leader the black community needs." His clothes and his demeanor were ridiculed (my husband was asked by *Esquire* to do a piece predicated on interviewing Sharpton while he was having his hair processed), his motives derided, and his tactics, which were those of an extremely sophisticated player who counted being widely despised among his stronger cards, not very well understood.

Whites tended to believe, and to say, that Sharpton was "using" the racial issue—which, in the sense that all political action is based on "using" one issue or another, he clearly was. Whites also tended to see him as destructive and irresponsible, indifferent to the truth or to the sensibilities of whites—which, most notoriously in the nurturing of the Tawana Brawley case, a primal fantasy in which white men were accused of a crime Sharpton may well have known to be a fabrication, he also clearly was. What seemed not at all understood was that for Sharpton, who had no interest in making the problem appear more tractable ("The question is, do you want to 'ease' it or do you want to 'heal' it," he had said when asked if his marches had not worked against "easing tension" in Bensonhurst), the fact that blacks and whites could sometimes be shown to have divergent interests by no means suggested the need for an ameliorative solution. Such divergent interests were instead a lucky break, a ready-made organizing tool, a dramatic illustration of who had the power and who did not, who was making it and who was falling below the line; a metaphor for the sense of victimization felt not only by blacks but by all those Sharpton called "the left-out opposition." *We got the power,* the chants go on "Sharpton and Fulani in Babylon: Volume I, The Battle of New York City," a tape of the speeches of Sharpton and Lenora Fulani, a leader of the New Alliance Party. *We are the chosen people. Out of the pain. We that can't even talk together. Have learned to walk together.*

"I'm no longer sure what I thought about Al Sharpton a year or two ago still applies," Jerry Nachman, the editor of the *New York Post,* who had frequently criticized Sharpton, told Howard Kurtz of the *Washington Post* in September of 1990. "I spent a lot of time on the street. There's a lot of anger, a lot of frustration. Rightly or wrongly, he may be articulating a great deal more of what typical attitudes are than some of us thought." Wilbert Tatum, the editor and publisher of the *Amsterdam News,* tried to explain to Kurtz how, in his view, Sharpton had been cast as "a caricature of black leadership":

> He was fat. He wore jogging suits. He wore a medallion and gold chains. And the unforgivable of unforgivables, he had processed hair. The white media, perhaps not consciously, said, "We're going to promote this guy because we can point up the ridiculousness and paucity of black leadership." Al understood precisely what they were doing, precisely. Al is probably the most brilliant tactician this country has ever produced . . .

Whites often mentioned, as a clinching argument, that Sharpton paid his demonstrators to appear; the figure usually mentioned was five dollars (by November 1990, when Sharpton was fielding demonstrators to protest the killing of a black woman alleged to have grabbed a police nightstick in the aftermath of a domestic dispute, a police source quoted in the *Post* had jumped the payment to twenty dollars), but the figure floated by a prosecutor on the jogger case was four dollars. This seemed on many levels a misunderstanding, or an estrangement, or as blacks would say a disrespect, too deep to address, but on its simplest level it served to suggest what value was placed by whites on what they thought of as black time.

In the fall of 1990, the fourth and fifth of the six defendants in the Central Park attack, Kevin Richardson and Kharey Wise, went on trial. Since this particular narrative had achieved full resolution, or catharsis, with the conviction of the first three defendants, the city's interest in the case had by then largely waned. Those "charlatans" who had sought to "exploit" the case had been whisked, until they could next prove useful, into the wings. Even the verdicts in this second trial, coinciding as they did with yet another arrest of John ("The Dapper Don") Gotti, a reliable favorite on the New York stage, did not lead the local news. It was in fact the economy itself that had come center stage in the city's new, and yet familiar, narrative work: a work in which the vital yet beleaguered city would or would not weather yet another "crisis" (the answer was a resounding yes); a work, or a dreamwork, that emphasized not only the cyclical nature of such "crises" but the regenerative power of the city's "contrasts." "With its migratory population, its diversity of cultures and institutions, and its vast resources of infrastructure, capital, and intellect, New York has been the quintessential modern city for more than a century, constantly reinventing itself," Michael Stone concluded in his

New York magazine cover story, "Hard Times." "Though the process may be long and painful, there's no reason to believe it won't happen again."

These were points commonly made in support of a narrative that tended, with its dramatic line of "crisis" and resolution, or recovery, only to further obscure the economic and historical groundwork for the situation in which the city found itself: that long unindictable conspiracy of criminal and semicriminal civic and commercial arrangements, deals, negotiations, gimmes and getmes, graft and grift, pipe, topsoil, concrete, garbage; the conspiracy of those in the know, those with a connection, those with a rabbi at the Department of Sanitation or the Buildings Department or the School Construction Authority or Foley Square, the conspiracy of those who believed everybody got upside down because of who it was, it happened to anybody else, a summons gets issued and that's the end of it. On November 12, 1990, in its page-one analysis of the city's troubles, the *New York Times* went so far as to locate, in "public spending," not the drain on the city's vitality and resources it had historically been but "an important positive factor":

> Not in decades has so much money gone for public works in the area—airports, highways, bridges, sewers, subways and other projects. Roughly $12 billion will be spent in the metropolitan region in the current fiscal year. Such government outlays are a healthy counterforce to a 43 percent decline since 1987 in the value of new private construction, a decline related to the sharp drop in real estate prices. . . . While nearly every industry in the pri-

vate sector has been reducing payrolls since spring, government hiring has risen, maintaining an annual growth rate of 20,000 people since 1987 . . .

That there might well be, in a city in which the proliferation of and increase in taxes were already driving private-sector payrolls out of town, hardly anyone left to tax for such public works and public-sector jobs was a point not too many people wished seriously to address: among the citizens of a New York come to grief on the sentimental stories told in defense of its own lazy criminality, the city's inevitability remained the given, the heart, the first and last word on which all the stories rested. We love New York, the narrative promises, because it matches our energy level.

—1990

CLINTON AGONISTES

September 22, 1998

1

No one who ever passed through an American public high school could have watched William Jefferson Clinton running for office in 1992 and failed to recognize the familiar predatory sexuality of the provincial adolescent. The man was, Jesse Jackson said that year to another point, "nothing but an appetite." No one who followed his appearances on *The Road to the White House* on C-SPAN could have missed the reservoir of self-pity, the quickness to blame, the narrowing of the eyes, as in a wildlife documentary, when things did not go his way: a response so reliable that aides on Jerry Brown's 1992 campaign looked for situations in which it could be provoked. The famous tendency of the candidate to take a less than forthcoming approach to embarrassing questions had already been documented and discussed, most exhaustively in the matter of his 1969 draft status, and he remained the front-runner. The persistent but initially unpublished rumors about extramarital rovings had been, once Gennifer Flowers told her story to the *Star,* published and acknowledged, and he remained on his feet. "I have acknowledged wrongdoing," he had told America during his and his wife's rather premonitory *60 Minutes* appearances on Super Bowl Sunday of that year. "I have acknowledged causing pain in my marriage. I think most Americans who are watching this tonight, they'll know what we're saying, they'll get it, and they'll feel that we have been more than candid. And I think what the press has to decide is, are we going to engage in a game of gotcha?"

Nothing that is now known about the forty-second president of the United States, in other words, was not known before the New Hampshire primary in 1992. The implicit message in his August 1998 testimony to the Office of the Independent Counsel was not different in kind from that made explicit in January 1992: *I think most Americans who are watching this . . . they'll know what we're saying, they'll get it, and they'll feel that we have been more than candid.* By the time of the 1992 general election, the candidate was before us as he appears today: a more detailed and realized character than that presented in the Office of the Independent Counsel's oddly novelistic *Referral to the United States House of Representatives* but recognizably drawn to similar risk, voraciously needy, deeply fractured, and yet there, a force to contend with, a possessor of whatever manna accrues to those who have fought themselves and survived. The flaws already apparent in 1992 were by no means unreported, but neither, particularly in those parts of the country recently neutralized by their enshrinement as "the heartland," were they seized as occasions for rhetorical outrage. "With 16 million Americans unemployed, 40 million Americans without health care and 3 million Americans homeless, here's what we have to say about presidential aspirant Bill Clinton's alleged previous marital infidelity," the *Peoria Journal-Star* declared on its editorial page at the time of the *60 Minutes* appearance. "So what? And that's all."

There were those for whom the candidate's clear personal volatility suggested the possibility of a similar evanescence on matters of ideology or policy, but even the coastal opinion leaders seemed willing to grant him a *laissez-passer* on this question of sex: "To what degree, if any, is the private action relevant to the duties of the public office?" the *Los Angeles Times* asked on its editorial page in January 1992. "Shouldn't our right to know about a candidate's sex life be confined . . . to offenses such as rape, harassment, or sex discrimination?" *The New York Times* report on the *60 Minutes* interview, which appeared on page A14 and was headlined "Clinton Defends His Privacy and Says the Press Intruded," was followed the next day by an editorial ("Leers, Smears and Governor Clinton") not only commending the candidate for having drawn a line "between idle curiosity and responsible attention" but noting that "he won't provide details and he need not, unless it develops that his private conduct arguably touches his public performance or fitness for office." The same day, January 28, 1992, A. M. Rosenthal wrote in the *Times* that Governor and Mrs. Clinton had "presented to the American public a gift and a lasting opportunity":

> The gift is that they treated us as adults. The opportunity is for us to act that way. . . . We can at least treasure the hope that Americans would be fed up with the slavering inquisition on politicians' sexual history and say to hell with that and the torturers. That would be a thank-you card worthy of the gift from the Clinton couple—the presumption that Americans have achieved adulthood, at last.

Few in the mainstream press, in 1992, demanded a demonstration of "contrition" from the candidate. Few, in 1992, demanded "full remorse," a doubtful concept even in those venues, courtrooms in which criminal trials have reached the penalty phase, where "remorse" is most routinely invoked. Few, in 1992, spoke of the United States as so infantilized as to require a president above the possibility of personal reproach. That so few did this then, and so many have done this since, has been construed by some as evidence that the interests and priorities of the press have changed. In fact the interests and priorities of the press have remained reliably the same: then as now, the press could be relied upon to report a rumor or a hint down to the ground (tree it, bag it, defoliate the forest for it, destroy the village for it), but only insofar as that rumor or hint gave promise of advancing the story of the day, the shared narrative, the broad line of whatever story was at the given moment commanding the full resources of the reporters covering it and the columnists commenting on it and the on-tap experts analyzing it on the talk shows. (The 1998 *Yearbook of Experts, Authorities & Spokespersons* tellingly provides, for producers with underdeveloped Rolodexes of their own, 1,477 telephone numbers to call for those guests "who will drive the news issues in the next year.") In *Spin Cycle,* a book in which Howard Kurtz of *The Washington Post* endeavored to show the skill of the "Clinton propaganda machine" (similarly described by Joe Klein, despite what might seem impressive evidence to the contrary, as "the most sophisticated communications apparatus in the history of American politics") at setting the agenda for the press, there appears this apparently ingenuous description of how the press itself sets its agenda:

> A front-page exclusive would ripple through the rest of the press corps, dominate the briefing, and most likely end up on the network news. The newsmagazine reporters were not quite as influential as in years past, but they could still change the dialogue or cement the conventional wisdom with a cover story or a behind-the-scenes report. Two vital groups of reinforcements backed up the White House regulars. . . . One was the columnists and opinion-mongers—Jonathan Alter at *Newsweek,* Joe Klein at *The New Yorker,* William Safire and Maureen Dowd at *The New York Times,* E. J. Dionne and Richard Cohen at *The Washington Post*—who could quickly change the zeitgeist. . . . the other was the dogged band of investigative reporters—Jeff Gerth at the *Times,* Bob Woodward at the *Post,* Glenn Simpson at *The Wall Street Journal,* Alan Miller at the *Los Angeles Times.*

Once the "zeitgeist" has been agreed upon by this quite small group of people, any unrelated event, whatever its actual significance, becomes either non-news or, if sufficiently urgent, a news brief. An example of the relegation to non-news would be this: Robert Scheer, in his *Los Angeles Times* review of *Spin Cycle,* noted that its index included eighteen references to Paula Jones and sixteen to John Huang, but none to Saddam Hussein. An example of the relegation to news brief would be this: on August 16, 1998, after hearing flash updates on the Omagh bombing in Northern Ireland ("worst attack in almost thirty years of violence . . . latest figures as we have it are 28 people dead . . . 220 people injured . . . 103 still in hospital") and on the American embassy bombings in East Africa, Wolf Blitzer, on a two-hour *Late Edition with Wolf Blitzer* otherwise exclusively devoted to the "legal ramifications, political considerations, and historic consequences" of Monica Lewinsky, said this: "Catherine Bond, reporting live from Nairobi, thanks for joining us. Turning now to the story that has all of Washington holding its breath . . ."

In 1992, as in any election year, the story that had all of Washington holding its breath was the campaign, and since the guardians of the zeitgeist, taking their cue from the political professionals, had early on certified Governor Clinton as the most electable of the Democratic candidates, his personal failings could serve only as a step in his quest, a test of his ability to prevail. Before the New

Hampshire primary campaign was even underway, Governor Clinton was reported to be the Democratic candidate with "centrist credentials," the Democratic candidate who "offered an assessment of the state of the American economy that borrows as much from Republicans like Jack Kemp as it does from liberals," the Democratic candidate who could go to California and win support from "top Republican fundraisers," the candidate, in short, who "scored well with party officials and strategists." A survey of Democratic National Committee members had shown Clinton in the lead. The late Ronald H. Brown, at the time chairman of the Democratic Party, had been reported, still before a single vote was cast in New Hampshire, to have pressured Mario Cuomo to remove his name from the New York primary ballot, so that a divisive favorite-son candidacy would not impede the chosen front-runner.

By the morning of January 26, 1992, the Sunday of the *60 Minutes* appearance and shortly after the candidate sealed his centrist credentials by allowing the execution of the brain-damaged Rickey Ray Rector to proceed in Arkansas, William Schneider, in the *Los Angeles Times,* was awarding Governor Clinton the coveted "Big Mo," noting that "the Democratic Party establishment is falling in line behind Clinton." In a party that reserves a significant percentage of its convention votes (eighteen percent in 1996) for "superdelegates," the seven-hundred-some elected and party officials not bound by any popular vote, the message sent by this early understanding among the professionals was clear, as it had been when the professionals settled on Michael Dukakis in 1988: the train was now leaving the station, and, since the campaign, as "story," requires that the chosen candidates be seen as contenders who will go the distance, all inconvenient baggage, including "the character issue," would be left on the platform. What would go on the train was what Joe Klein, echoing the note of romantic credulity in his own 1992 coverage of the candidate Bill Clinton (that was before the zeitgeist moved on), recalled in 1998 in *The New Yorker* as the "precocious fizz" of the War Room, "the all-nighters . . . about policy or philosophy," the candidate who "loved to talk about serious things" and "seems to be up on every social program in America."

2

It was January 16, 1998, when Kenneth W. Starr obtained authorization, by means of a court order opaquely titled "*In re* Madison Guaranty Savings & Loan Association," to extend his languishing Whitewater inquiry to the matter of Monica Lewinsky. It was also January 16 when Monica Lewinsky was detained for eleven hours and twenty-five minutes in Room 1016 of the Ritz-Carlton Hotel in Pentagon City, Virginia, where, according to the independent counsel's log of the "meeting," the FBI agent who undertook to read Miss Lewinsky "her rights as found on the form FD-395, Interrogation, Advice of Rights" was, for reasons the log does not explain, "unable to finish reading the FD-395." Miss Lewinsky herself testified:

Then Jackie Bennett [of the Office of the Independent Counsel] came in and there was a whole bunch of other people and the room was crowded and he was saying to me, you know, you have to make a decision. I had wanted to call my mom, they weren't going to let me call my attorney, so I just—I wanted to call my mom and they— Then Jackie Bennett said, "You're 24, you're smart, you're old enough, you don't need to call your mommy."

It was January 17 when President Clinton, in the course of giving his deposition in the civil suit brought against him by Paula Corbin Jones, either did or did not spring the perjury trap that Kenneth Starr either had or had not set. By the morning of January 21, when both Susan Schmidt in *The Washington Post* and ABC News correspondent Jackie Judd on *Good Morning America* jumped the stakes by quoting "sources" saying that Monica Lewinsky was on tape with statements that the president and Vernon Jordan had told her to lie, the "character issue" had gone from idle to full throttle, with Sam Donaldson and George Stephanopoulos and Jonathan Alter already on air talking about "impeachment proceedings."

In most discussions of how and why this matter came so incongruously to escalate, the press of course was criticized, and was in turn quick to criticize itself (or, in the phrasing preferred by many, since it suggested that any objection rested on hairsplitting, to "flagellate" itself), citing excessive and in some cases erroneous coverage. Perhaps because not all of the experts, authorities, and spokespersons driving this news had extensive experience with the kind of city-side beat on which it is taken for granted that the D.A.'s office will leak the cases they doubt they can make, selective prosecutorial hints had become embedded in the ongoing story as fact. "Loose attribution of sources abounded," Jules Witcover wrote in the March/April 1998 *Columbia Journalism Review,* although, since he intended to attribute the most egregious examples to "journalistic amateurs" and "journalistic pretenders" (Arianna Huffington and Matt Drudge), he could still express "hope," based on what he discerned two months into the story as "a tapering off of the mad frenzy of the first week or so," that, among "established, proven professional practitioners," any slip had been "a mere lapse of standards in the heat of a fast-breaking, incredibly competitive story of major significance."

For the same *CJR,* the cover line of which was "Where We Went Wrong . . . and What We Do Now," a number of other reporters, editors, and news executives were queried, and expressed similar hopes. The possibility of viewer confusion between entertainment and news shows was mentioned. The necessity for more careful differentiation among different kinds of leaks was mentioned. The "new technology" and "hypercompetition" and "the speed of news cycles these days" were mentioned, references to the way in which the Internet and the multiplication of cable channels had collapsed the traditional cyclical presentation of news into a twenty-four-hour stream of provisional raw takes. "We're in a new world in terms of the way information flows to the nation," James O'Shea, deputy managing editor for news of the *Chicago Tribune,* said. (The Lewinsky story had in fact first broken not in the traditional media but on the Internet, in a

1:11 A.M. January 18, 1998, posting on the *Drudge Report*.) "The days when you can decide not to print a story because it's not well enough sourced are long gone. When a story gets into the public realm, as it did with the *Drudge Report,* then you have to characterize it, you have to tell your readers, 'This is out there, you've probably been hearing about it on TV and the Internet. We have been unable to substantiate it independently.' And then give them enough information to judge the validity of it."

That the "story" itself might in this case be anything other than (in Witcover's words) "a fast-breaking, incredibly competitive story of major significance" was questioned by only one panelist, Anthony Lewis of *The New York Times,* who characterized "the obsession of the press with sex and public officials" as "crazy," but allowed that "after Linda Tripp went to the prosecutor, it became hard to say we shouldn't be covering this." The more general attitude seemed to be that there might have been an excess here or an error there, but the story itself was important by definition, significant because it was commanding the full resources of everyone on it—not unlike a campaign, which this story, in that it offered a particularly colorful version of the personalized "horse race" narrative that has become the model for most American political reporting, in fact resembled. "This is a very valid story of a strong-willed prosecutor and a president whose actions have been legitimately questioned," Walter Isaacson of *Time* said. "A case involving sex can be a very legitimate story, but we can't let our journalistic standards lapse simply because the sexual element makes everyone overexcited."

This, then, was a story "involving sex," a story in which there was a "sexual element," but, as we so frequently heard, it was not about sex, just as Whitewater, in the words of one of the several score editorials to this point published over the years by *The Wall Street Journal,* was "not merely about a land deal." What both stories were about, of course (although in the absence of both sex and evidence against the president one of them had proved a harder sell), was which of the contenders, the "strong-willed prosecutor" or his high-placed target, would go the distance, win the race. "The next forty-eight to seventy-two hours are critical," Tim Russert was saying on January 21, 1998, on MSNBC, where the daily recalibration of such sudden-death scenarios would by August raise the cable's Nielsen households from 49,000 a year before to 197,000. "I think his presidency is numbered in days," Sam Donaldson was saying by Sunday of the same week.

"On the high-status but low-interest White House beat, there is no story as exciting as that of the fall of a president," Jacob Weisberg observed in *Slate* in March. The president, everyone by then agreed, was "toast." The president "had to go," or "needed to go." The reasons the president needed to go had seemed, those last days in January and into February, crisp, easy to explain, grounded as they were in the galvanizing felony prospects set adrift without attribution by the Office of the Independent Counsel: obstruction of justice, subornation of perjury. Then, as questions threatened to slow the story (Would it not be unusual to prosecute someone for perjury in a civil suit? Did the chronology present a circumstantial case for, or actually against, obstruction? If someone lied in a deposition about a matter later ruled not essential to and so inadmissible in the case at hand, as Lewinsky had been ruled in *Jones v. Clinton,* was it in fact perjury?), the reasons the president "needed to go" became less crisp, more subjective, more a matter of "the mood here in the capital," and so, by definition, less open to argument from those not there in the capital.

This story was definitely moving, as they kept saying on MSNBC. By April 1, 1998, when U.S. District Court Judge Susan Webber Wright rendered the possibility of any felony technically remote by dismissing *Jones v. Clinton* altogether, the story had already rolled past its inconvenient legal (or "legalistic," a much-used word by then) limitations: ten weeks after America first heard the name Monica Lewinsky and still in the absence of any allegation bearing on the president's performance of his duties, the reasons the president needed to go were that he had been "weakened," that he would be "unable to function." The president's own former chief of staff, Leon Panetta, had expressed concern about "the slow drip-drip process and the price he's paying in terms of his ability to lead the country." When the congressional staff members were asked in late March 1998 where they believed the situation was leading, twenty-one percent of Democratic staff members (forty-three percent of Republican) had foreseen, in the absence of resignation, impeachment proceedings.

The story was positioned, in short, for the satisfying long haul. By August 17, 1998, when the president con-

firmed the essential fact in the testimony Monica Lewinsky had given the grand jury eleven days before, virtually
every "news analyst" on the eastern seaboard was on air
(we saw the interiors of many attractive summer houses)
talking about "the president's credibility," about "can he
lead" or "still govern in any reasonably effective manner,"
questions most cogently raised that week by Garry Wills
in *Time* and, to a different point, by Thomas L. Friedman
in *The New York Times*. Proceeding from a belief both in
President Clinton's underlying honor and in the redemp-
tive power, if he was to be faced by crippling harassment,
of the "principled resignation," Wills had tried to locate
the homiletic possibilities in the dilemma, the opportunities for spiritual growth that could accrue to the country
and to the president through resignation. The divergence
between this argument and that made by Friedman was
instructive. Friedman had seemed to be offering "can he
lead" mainly as a strategy, an argument with which the
professionals of the political process, who were increasingly bewildered by the public's apparent disinclination to
join the rush to judgment by then general in the columns
and talk shows, might most adroitly reeducate that "sub-
stantial majority" who "still feel that Mr. Clinton should
remain in office."

In other words we had arrived at a dispiriting and familiar point, and would be fated to remain there even as
telephone logs and Epass Access Control Reports and
pages of grand-jury testimony floated down around us:
"the disconnect," as it was now called, between what the

professionals—those who held public office, those who worked for them, and those who wrote about them—believed to be self-evident and what a majority of Americans believed to be self-evident. John Kennedy and Warren Harding had both conducted affairs in the Oval Office (more recently known as "the workplace," or "under the same roof where his daughter lay sleeping"), and these affairs were by no means the largest part of what Americans thought about either of them. "If you step back a bit, it still doesn't look like a constitutional crisis," former federal prosecutor E. Lawrence Barcella told the *Los Angeles Times* to this point. "This is still a case about whether the President had sex with someone half his age. The American people have understood—certainly better than politicians, lawyers, and the press—that if this is ultimately about sex, it's really no one else's business. There are acceptable lies and unacceptable lies, and lying about someone's sex life is one of those tolerated lies."

Ten days after the president's August 17 admission to the nation, or ten days into the endless tape loop explicating the inadequacies of that admission, Mr. Clinton's own polls, according to *The Washington Post,* showed pretty much what everyone else's polls showed and would continue to show, notwithstanding the release first of Kenneth Starr's "narrative" and "grounds for impeachment" and then of Mr. Clinton's videotaped testimony and 3,183 pages of "supporting documents": that a majority of the public had believed all along that the president had some kind of involvement with Monica Lewinsky ("Cheat once, cheat twice, there's probably a whole line of them," a thirty-four-year-old woman told Democratic pollster Peter Hart in a focus session attended by the *Los Angeles Times*) continued to see it as a private rather than a political matter, believed Kenneth Starr to be the kind of sanctimonious hall monitor with sex on the brain they had avoided in their formative years (as in the jump-rope rhyme *Rooty-toot-toot! Rooty-toot-toot! / There go the boys from the Institute! / They don't smoke and they don't chew / And they don't go with the girls who do*), and, even as they acknowledged the gravity of lying under oath, did not wish to see the president removed from office.

The charge that he tried to conceal a personally embarrassing but not illegal liaison had not, it seemed, impressed most Americans as serious. Whether or not he had ever asked Vernon Jordan to call Ron Perelman and whether Vernon Jordan had in fact done so before or after the subpoena was issued to Monica Lewinsky had not, it seemed, much mattered to these citizens. Outside the capital, there had seemed to be a general recognition that the entire "crisis," although mildly entertaining, represented politics as usual, particularly since it had evolved from a case, the 1994 *Jones v. Clinton,* that would probably never have been brought and certainly never been funded had Mr. Clinton not been elected president. For Thomas L. Friedman, then, the way around this was to produce more desirable polling results by refocusing the question, steering the issue safely past the shoals of "should he be president," which was the essence of what the research was asking. "What might influence the public most," Friedman wrote, "is the question of 'can' Mr. Clinton still govern in any reasonably effective manner."

Since taking this argument to its logical conclusion raised, for a public demonstrably impatient with what it had come to see as a self-interested political class, certain other questions (If the president couldn't govern, who wouldn't let him? Was it likely that they would have let a lame duck govern anyway? What in fact was "governing," and did we want it?), most professionals fell back to a less vulnerable version of what the story was: a story so simple, so sentimental, as to brook no argument, no talking back from "the American people," who were increasingly seen as recalcitrant children, fecklessly resistant to responsible guidance. The story, William J. Bennett told us on *Meet the Press,* was about the "moral and intellectual disarmament" that befalls a nation when its president is not "being a decent example" and "teaching the kids the difference between right and wrong." The story, Cokie Roberts told us in the *New York Daily News,* was about reinforcing the lesson "that people who act immorally and lie get punished." The story, William Kristol told us on *This Week,* was about the president's "defiance," his "contempt," his "refusal to acknowledge some standards of public morality."

Certain pieties were repeated to the point where they could be referred to in shorthand. Although most Americans had an instinctive sense that Monica Lewinsky could well have been, as the *Referral* would later reveal her to have been, a less than entirely passive participant in whatever happened, we heard about the situational inviolability of interns (interns were "given into our care," interns were "lent to us by their parents") until Cokie Roberts's censorious cry to an insufficiently outraged congress-woman ("But with an *intern?*") could stand alone, a ver-dict that required no judge or jury. We heard repeatedly about "our children," or "our kids," who were, as pre-sented, avid consumers of the *Nightly News* in whose presence sex had never before been mentioned and dis-cussions of the presidency were routine. "I'd like to be able to tell my children, 'You should tell the truth,'" Stu-art Taylor of the *National Journal* told us on *Meet the Press.* "I'd like to be able to tell them, 'You should respect the president.' And I'd like to be able to tell them both things at the same time." Jonathan Alter, in *Newsweek,* spoke of the president as someone "who has made it virtually impossible to talk to your kids about the American presi-dency or let them watch the news."

"I approach this as a mother," Cokie Roberts said on *This Week.* "We have a right to say to this president, 'What you have done is an example to our children that's a disgrace,'" William J. Bennett said on *Meet the Press.* The apparent inability of the public to grasp this *Kinder-Kirche* point (perhaps because not all Americans could afford the luxury of idealizing their own children) had itself become an occasion for outrage and scorn: the public was too "complacent," or too "prosperous," or too "fixed on the Dow Jones." The public in fact became the unindicted co-conspirator: "This ought to be something that outrages us, makes us ashamed of him," Mona Charen complained on *Late Edition with Wolf Blitzer.* "This casts shame on the entire country because he behaved that way and all of the

nation seems to be complicit now because they aren't rising up in righteous indignation."

This was the impasse (or, as it turned out, the box
canyon) that led many into a scenario destined to prove
wishful at best: "The American people," we heard repeatedly, would cast off their complicity when they were
actually forced by the report of the independent counsel
to turn their attention from the Dow and face what
Thomas L. Friedman, in the *Times,* called "the sordid
details that will come out from Ken Starr's investigation."
"People are not as sophisticated as this appears to be,"
William Kristol had said hopefully the day before the
president's televised address. "We all know, inside the
Beltway, what's in that report," Republican strategist Mary
Matalin said. "And I don't think . . . the country needs to
hear any more about tissue, dresses, cigars, ties, anything
else." George Will, on *This Week,* assured his co-panelists
that support for the president would evaporate in the face
of the *Referral.* "Because Ken Starr must—the president
has forced his hand—must detail graphically the sexual
activity that demonstrates his perjury. Once that report is
written and published, Congress will be dragged along in
the wake of the public. . . . Once the dress comes in, and
some of the details come in from the Ken Starr report,
people—there's going to be a critical mass, the yuck factor—where people say, 'I don't want him in my living
room anymore.'"

The person most people seemed not to want in their
living rooms any more was "Ken" (as he was now called
by those with an interest in protecting his story), but this
itself was construed as evidence of satanic spin on the part

of the White House. "The president's men," William J. Bennett cautioned in *The Death of Outrage: Bill Clinton and the Assault on American Ideals,* ". . . attempt relentlessly to portray their opposition as bigoted and intolerant fanatics who have no respect for privacy." He continued:

> At the same time they offer a temptation to their sup-
> porters: the temptation to see themselves as realists,
> worldly-wise, sophisticated: in a word, European. This
> temptation should be resisted by the rest of us. In Amer-
> ica, morality is central to our politics and attitudes in a
> way that is not the case in Europe, and precisely this
> moral streak is what is best about us. . . . Europeans may
> have something to teach us about, say, wine or haute
> couture. But on the matter of morality in politics, Amer-
> ica has much to teach Europe.

American innocence itself, then, was now seen to hang on the revealed word of the *Referral.* The report, Fox News promised, would detail "activities that most Amer-icans would describe as unusual." These details, *Newsweek* promised, would make Americans "want to throw up." "Specifics about a half-dozen sex acts," *Newsday* prom-ised, had been provided "during an unusual two-hour session August 26 in which Lewinsky gave sworn testi-mony in Starr's downtown office, not before the grand jury."

This is arresting, and not to be brushed over. On August 6, Monica Lewinsky had told the grand jury that sexual acts had occurred. On August 17, the president had tacitly confirmed this in both his testimony to the grand jury and his televised address to the nation. Given this sequence, the "unusual two-hour session August 26" might have seemed, to some, unnecessary, even excessive, not least because of the way in which, despite the full knowledge of the prosecutors that the details elicited in this session would be disseminated to the world in two weeks under the *Referral* headings "November 15 Sexual Encounter," "November 17 Sexual Encounter," "December 31 Sexual Encounter," "January 7 Sexual Encounter," "January 21 Sexual Encounter," "February 4 Sexual Encounter and Subsequent Phone Calls," "March 31 Sexual Encounter," "Easter Telephone Conversations and Sexual Encounter," "February 28 Sexual Encounter," and "March 29 Sexual Encounter," certain peculiar and warped proprieties had been so pruriently observed. "In deference to Lewinsky and the explicit nature of her testimony," *Newsday* reported, "all the prosecutors, defense lawyers and stenographers in the room during the session were women."

Since the "explicit nature of the testimony," the "unusual activity," the "throw-up details" everyone seemed to know about (presumably because they had been leaked by the Office of the Independent Counsel) turned out to involve masturbation, it was hard not to wonder if those in the know might not be experiencing some sort of rhetorical autointoxication, a kind of rapture of the feed. The average age of first sexual intercourse in this country has been for some years sixteen, and is younger in many venues. Since the average age of first marriage in this country is twenty-five for women and twenty-seven for men, sexual activity outside marriage occurs among

Americans for an average of nine to eleven years. Six out of ten marriages in this country are likely to end in divorce, a significant percentage of those who divorce doing so after engaging in extramarital sexual activity. As of the date of the 1990 census, there were in this country 4.1 million households headed by unmarried couples. More than thirty-five percent of these households included children. Seventh-graders in some schools in this country were as early as the late 1970s reading the Boston Women's Health Book Collective's *Our Bodies, Ourselves,* which explained the role of masturbation in sexuality and the use of foreign objects in masturbation. The notion that Americans apparently willing to overlook a dalliance in the Oval Office would go pale at its rather commonplace details seemed puzzling in the extreme, as did the professed inability to understand why these Americans might favor the person who had engaged in a common sexual act over the person who had elicited the details of that act as evidence for a public stoning.

But of course these members of what Howard Fineman recently defined on MSNBC as "the national political class," the people "who read the *Hotline* or watch cable television political shows such as this one," were not talking about Americans at large. They did not know Americans at large. They occasionally heard from one, in a focus group or during the Q&A after a lecture date, but their attention, since it was focused on the political process, which had come to represent the concerns not of the country at large but of the organized pressure groups that increasingly controlled it, remained remote. When Howard Fineman, during the same MSNBC appearance, spoke of "the full-scale panic" that he detected "both here in Washington and out around the country," he was referring to calls he had made to "a lot of Democratic consultants, pollsters, media people and so forth," as well as to candidates: "For example one in Wisconsin, a woman running for the Democratic seat up there, she said she's beginning to get calls and questions from average folks wanting to know what her view of Bill Clinton is."

"Average folks," however, do not call their elected representatives, nor do they attend the events where the funds get raised and the questions asked. The citizens who do are the citizens with access, the citizens with an investment, the citizens who have a special interest. When Representative Tom Coburn (R-Okla.) reported to *The Washington Post* that during three days in September 1998 he received five hundred phone calls and 850 e-mails on the question of impeachment, he would appear to have been reporting, for the most part, less on "average folks" than on constituents who already knew, or had been provided, his telephone number or e-mail address; reporting, in other words, on an organized blitz campaign. When Gary Bauer of the Family Research Council seized the moment by test-running a drive for the presidency with a series of Iowa television spots demanding Mr. Clinton's resignation, he would appear to have been interested less in reaching out to "average folks" than in galvanizing certain caucus voters, the very caucus voters who might be expected to have already called or e-mailed Washington on the question of impeachment.

When these people on the political talk shows spoke about the inability of Americans to stomach "the details," then, they were speaking, in code, about a certain kind of American, a minority of the population but the minority to whom recent campaigns have been increasingly pitched. They were talking politics. They were talking about the "values" voter, the "pro-family" voter, and so complete by now was their isolation from the country in which they lived that they seemed willing to reserve its franchise for, in other words give it over to, that key core vote.

3

The cost of producing a television show on which Wolf Blitzer or John Gibson referees an argument between an unpaid "former federal prosecutor" and an unpaid "legal scholar" is significantly lower than that of producing conventional programming. This is, as they say, the "end of the day," or the bottom-line fact. The explosion of "news comment" programming occasioned by this fact requires, if viewers are to be kept from tuning out, nonstop breaking stories on which the stakes can be raised hourly. The Gulf War made CNN, but it was the trial of O. J. Simpson that taught the entire broadcast industry how to perfect the pushing of the stakes. The crisis that led to the Clinton impeachment began as and remained a situation in which a handful of people, each of whom believed that he or she had something to gain (a book contract, a scoop, a sinecure as a network "analyst," contested ground in the culture wars, or, in the case of Starr, the justification of his failure to get either of the Clintons on Whitewater), managed to harness this phenomenon and ride it. This was not an unpredictable occurrence, nor was it unpredictable that the rather impoverished but generally unremarkable transgressions in question would come in this instance to be inflated by the rhetoric of moral rearmament.

"You cannot defile the temple of justice," Kenneth Starr told reporters during his many front-lawn and driveway appearances. "There's no room for white lies. There's no room for shading. There's only room for truth. . . . Our job is to determine whether crimes were committed." This was the authentic if lonely voice of the last American wilderness, the voice of the son of a Texas preacher in a fundamentalist denomination (the Churches of Christ) so focused on the punitive that it forbade even the use of instrumental music in church. This was the voice of a man who himself knew a good deal about risk-taking, an Ahab who had been mortified by his great Whitewater whale and so in his pursuit of what Melville called "the highest truth" would submit to the House, despite repeated warnings from his own supporters (most visibly on the editorial page of *The Wall Street Journal*) not to do so, a report in which his attempt to take down the government was based in its entirety on ten occasions of backseat intimacy as detailed by an eager but unstable participant who appeared to have memorialized the events on her hard drive.

This was a curious document. It was reported by *The New York Times,* on the day after its initial and partial release, to have been written in part by Stephen Bates, identified as a "part-time employee of the independent counsel's office and the part-time literary editor of the *Wilson Quarterly*," an apparent polymath who after his 1987 graduation from Harvard Law School "wrote for publications as diverse as *The Nation, The Weekly Standard, Playboy,* and *The New Republic.*" According to the *Times,* Mr. Bates and Mr. Starr had together written a proposal for a book about a high school student in Omaha barred by her school from forming a Bible study group. The proposed book, which did not find a publisher, was to be titled *Bridget's Story.* This is interesting, since the "narrative" section of the *Referral,* including as it does a wealth of nonrelevant or "story" details (for example, the threatening letter from Miss Lewinsky to the president that the president said he had not read, although "Ms. Lewinsky suspected that he had actually read the whole thing"), seems very much framed as "Monica's Story." We repeatedly share her "feelings," just as we might have shared Bridget's: "I left that day sort of emotionally stunned," Miss Lewinsky is said to have testified at one point, for "I just knew he was in love with me."

Consider this. The day in question, July 4, 1997, was six weeks after the most recent of the president's attempts to break off their relationship. The previous day, after weeks of barraging members of the White House staff with messages and calls detailing her frustration at being unable to reach the president, her conviction that he owed her a job, and her dramatically good intentions ("I know that in your eyes I am just a hindrance—a woman who doesn't have a certain someone's best interests at

heart, but please trust me when I say I do"), Miss Lewinsky had dispatched a letter that "obliquely," as the narrative has it, "threatened to disclose their relationship." On
this day, July 4, the president has at last agreed to see her.
He accuses her of threatening him. She accuses him of failing to secure for her an appropriate job, which in fact she
would define in a later communiqué as including "anything at *George* magazine." "The most important things to
me," she would then specify, "are that I am engaged and
interested in my work, I am *not* someone's administrative/
executive assistant, and my salary can provide me with a
comfortable living in NY."

At this point she cried. He "praised her intellect and
beauty," according to the narrative. He said, according to
Miss Lewinsky, "he wished he had more time for me."
She left the Oval Office, "emotionally stunned," con-
vinced "he was in love with me." The "narrative," in
other words, offers what is known among students of fiction as an unreliable first-person narrator, a classic literary
device whereby the reader is made to realize that the situation, and indeed the narrator, are other than what the
narrator says they are. It cannot have been the intention of
the authors to present their witness as the victimizer and
the president her hapless victim, and yet there it was, for
all the world to read. That the authors of the *Referral*
should have fallen into this basic craft error suggests the
extent to which, by the time the *Referral* was submitted,
the righteous voice of the grand inquisitor had isolated
itself from the more wary voices of his cannier allies.

That the voice of the inquisitor was not one to which large numbers of Americans would respond had always been, for these allies, beside the point: what it offered, and what less authentic voices obligingly amplified, was a platform for the reintroduction of fundamentalism, or "values issues," into the general discourse. "Most politicians miss the heart and soul of this concern," Ralph Reed wrote in 1996, having previously defined "the culture, the family, a loss of values, a decline in civility, and the destruction of our children" as the chief concerns of the Christian Coalition, which in 1996 claimed to have between a quarter and a third of its membership among registered Democrats. Despite two decades during which the promotion of the "values" agenda had been the common cause of both the "religious" (or Christian) and the neo-conservative right, too many politicians, Reed believed, still "debate issues like accountants." John Podhoretz, calling on Republicans in 1996 to resist the efforts of Robert Dole and Newt Gingrich to "de-ideologize" the Republican Party, had echoed, somewhat less forthrightly, Reed's complaint about the stress on economic issues. "They do not answer questions about the spiritual health of the nation," he wrote. "They do not address the ominous sense we all have that Americans are, with every intake of breath, unconsciously inhaling a philosophy that stresses individual pleasure over individual responsibility; that our capacity to be our best selves is weakening."

That "all" of us did not actually share this "ominous sense" was, again, beside the point, since neither Reed nor Podhoretz was talking about all of us. Less than fifty percent of the voting-age population in this country actually voted (for anyone) for president in 1996. The figures in the previous five presidential-year elections ranged from fifty to fifty-five percent. Only between thirty-three and thirty-eight percent voted in any midterm election since 1974. The figures for those who vote in primary elections, where the terms on which the campaign will be waged are determined, drop even further, in some cases into the single digits. Ralph Reed and John Podhoretz had been talking in 1996, as William Kristol and Mary Matalin would be talking in 1998, about that small group of citizens for whom "the spiritual health of the nation" would serve as the stalking horse for a variety of "social," or control-and-respect, issues. They were talking, in other words, about that narrow subsection of the electorate known in American politics as most-likely-to-vote.

What the Christian Coalition and *The Weekly Standard* were asking the Republican Party and (by logical extension) its opponents to do in 1996 was to further narrow most-likely-to-vote, by removing from debate those issues that concerned the country at large. This might have seemed, at the time, a ticket only to marginalization. It might have seemed, as recently as 1996, a rather vain hope that the nation's opinion leaders would soon reach general agreement that the rearming of the citizenry's moral life required that three centuries of legal precedent and even constitutional protections be overridden in the higher interest of demonstrating the presence of moral error, or "determining whether a crime has been committed," as Kenneth Starr put it in the brief he submitted to the Supreme Court in the matter of whether Vincent Foster's lawyer could be compelled to turn over notes on conversations he had with Foster before his death. Yet by August 1998, here were two of those opinion leaders, George Will and Cokie Roberts, stiffening the spines of those members of Congress who might be tempted to share the inclination of their constituents to distinguish between mortal and venial sins:

> *G.W.:* Cokie, the metastasizing corruption spread by this man [the president] is apparent now. And the corruption of the very idea of what it means to be a representative. We hear people in Congress saying, "Our job is solely to read the public opinion polls and conform thereto. Well, if so, that's not intellectually complicated, it's not morally demanding. But it makes a farce of being a . . .

> *C.R.:* No, at that point, we should just go for direct democracy.

> *G.W.:* Exactly. Get them out of here and let's plug computers in. . . .

> *C.R.:* . . . I must say I think that letting the [impeachment] process work makes a lot of sense because it brings—then people can lead public opinion rather than just follow it through the process.

> *G.W.:* What a concept.

> *G.R.:* But we will see.

To talk about the failure of Congress to sufficiently isolate itself from the opinion of the electorate as a "corruption of the very idea of what it means to be a representative" is to talk (another kind of "end of the day," or bottom-line fact) about disenfranchising America. "The public was fine, the elites were not," an unnamed White House adviser had told *The Washington Post* about the difference of opinion, on the matter of the president's "apology" or "nonapology," between the political professionals and what had until recently been deferrred to, if only pro forma, as the electorate. "You've got to let the elites win one."

No one should have doubted that the elites would in fact win this one, since, even before the somewhat dampening polling on the Starr report and on the president's videotaped testimony, the enterprise had achieved the perfect circularity toward which it had long been tending. "I want to find out who else in the political class thinks the way Mr. Clinton does about what is acceptable behavior," George Will had said in August, explaining why he favored impeachment proceedings over a resignation. "Let's smoke them out." That a majority of Americans seemed capable of separating Mr. Clinton's behavior in this matter from his performance as president had become, by that point, irrelevant, as had the ultimate outcome of the congressional deliberation. What was going to happen had already happened: since future elections could now be focused on the entirely spurious issue of correct sexual, or "moral," behavior, those elections would be increasingly decided by that committed and well-organized minority brought most reliably to the polls by "pro-family," or "values," issues. The fact that an election

between two candidates arguing which has the more correct "values" left most voters with no reason to come to
the polls had even come to be spoken about, by less wary
professionals, as the beauty part, the bonus that would
render the process finally and perpetually impenetrable.
"Who cares what every adult thinks?" a Republican strategist asked *The Washington Post* to this point in early September 1998. "It's totally not germane to this election."

—1998

FIXED OPINIONS,
OR THE HINGE OF HISTORY

*The following is based on a lecture given
November 2002 at the New York Public
Library.*

1

Seven days after September 11, 2001, I left New York
to do two weeks of book promotion, under other circumstances a predictable kind of trip. You fly into one
city or another, you do half an hour on local NPR, you
do a few minutes on drive-time radio, you do an "event,"
a talk or a reading or an onstage discussion. You sign
books, you take questions from the audience. You go
back to the hotel, order a club sandwich from room service, and leave a 5 A.M. call with the desk, so that in the
morning you can go back to the airport and fly to the
next city. During the week between September 11 and
the Wednesday morning when I went to Kennedy to get
on the plane, none of these commonplace aspects of
publishing a book seemed promising or even appropriate
things to be doing. But—like most of us who were in
New York that week—I was in a kind of protective
coma, sleepwalking through a schedule made when plan-

ning had still seemed possible. In fact I was protecting
myself so successfully that I had no idea how raw we all
were until that first night, in San Francisco, when I was
handed a book onstage and asked to read a few marked
lines from an essay about New York I had written in
1967.

Later I remembered thinking: 1967, no problem, no
land mines there.

I put on my glasses. I began to read.

"New York was no mere city," the marked lines began.
"It was instead an infinitely romantic notion, the myste-
rious nexus of all love and money and power, the shining
and perishable dream itself."

I hit the world "perishable" and I could not say it.

I found myself onstage at the Herbst Theater in San
Francisco unable to finish reading the passage, unable to
speak at all for what must have been thirty seconds. All I
can say about the rest of that evening, and about the two
weeks that followed, is that they turned out to be nothing
I had expected, nothing I had ever before experienced,
an extraordinarily open kind of traveling dialogue, an
encounter with an America apparently immune to conventional wisdom. The book I was making the trip to talk
about was *Political Fictions,* a series of pieces I had written
for *The New York Review* about the American political
process from the 1988 through the 2000 presidential elections. These people to whom I was listening—in San
Francisco and Los Angeles and Portland and Seattle—
were making connections I had not yet in my numbed
condition thought to make: connections between that
political process and what had happened on Septem-

ber 11, connections between our political life and the shape our reaction would take and was in fact already taking.

These people recognized that even then, within days after the planes hit, there was a good deal of opportunistic ground being seized under cover of the clearly urgent need for increased security. These people recognized even then, with flames still visible in lower Manhattan, that the words "bipartisanship" and "national unity" had come to mean acquiescence to the administration's preexisting agenda—for example the imperative for further tax cuts, the necessity for Arctic drilling, the systematic elimination of regulatory and union protections, even the funding for the missile shield—as if we had somehow missed noticing the recent demonstration of how limited, given a few box cutters and the willingness to die, superior technology can be.

These people understood that when Judy Woodruff, on the evening the president first addressed the nation, started talking on CNN about what "a couple of Democratic consultants" had told her about how the president would be needing to position himself, Washington was still doing business as usual. They understood that when the political analyst William Schneider spoke the same night about how the president had "found his vision thing," about how "this won't be the Bush economy anymore, it'll be the Osama bin Laden economy," Washington was still talking about the protection and perpetuation of its own interests.

These people got it.

They didn't like it.

They stood up in public and they talked about it.

Only when I got back to New York did I find that people, if they got it, had stopped talking about it. I came in from Kennedy to find American flags flying all over the Upper East Side, at least as far north as 96th Street, flags that had not been there in the first week after the fact. I say "at least as far north as 96th Street" because a few days later, driving down from Washington Heights past the big projects that would provide at least some of the manpower for the "war on terror" that the president had declared—as if terror were a state and not a technique—I saw very few flags: at most, between 168th Street and 96th Street, perhaps a half-dozen. There were that many flags on my building alone. Three at each of the two entrances. I did not interpret this as an absence of feeling for the country above 96th Street. I interpreted it as an absence of trust in the efficacy of rhetorical gestures.

There was much about this return to New York that I had not expected. I had expected to find the annihilating economy of the event—the way in which it had concentrated the complicated arrangements and misarrangements of the last century into a single irreducible image—being explored, made legible. On the contrary, I found that what had happened was being processed, obscured, systematically leached of history and so of meaning, finally rendered less readable than it had seemed on the morning it happened. As if overnight, the irreconcilable event had been made manageable, reduced to the sentimental, to protective talismans, totems, garlands of garlic, repeated pieties that would come to seem in some ways as destructive as the event itself. We now had "the loved ones," we had "the families," we had "the heroes."

In fact it was in the reflexive repetition of the word "hero" that we began to hear what would become in the year that followed an entrenched preference for ignoring the meaning of the event in favor of an impenetrably flattening celebration of its victims, and a troublingly belligerent idealization of historical ignorance. "Taste" and "sensitivity," it was repeatedly suggested, demanded that we not examine what happened. Images of the intact towers were already being removed from advertising, as if we might conveniently forget they had been there. The Roundabout Theatre had canceled a revival of Stephen Sondheim's *Assassins,* on the grounds that it was "not an appropriate time" to ask audiences "to think critically about various aspects of the American experience." The McCarter Theatre at Princeton had canceled a production of Richard Nelson's *The Vienna Notes,* which involves a terrorist act, saying that "it would be insensitive of us to present the play at this moment in our history."

I found in New York that "the death of irony" had already been declared, repeatedly, and curiously, since irony had been declared dead at the precise moment— given that the gravity of September 11 derived specifically from its designed implosion of historical ironies—when we might have seemed most in need of it. "One good thing could come from this horror: it could spell the end of the age of irony," Roger Rosenblatt wrote within days of the event in *Time,* a thought, or not a thought, destined to be frequently echoed but never explicated. Similarly, I found that "the death of postmodernism" had also been declared. ("It seemed bizarre that events so serious would be linked causally with a rarified form of academic talk," Stanley Fish wrote after receiving a call from a reporter asking if September 11 meant the end of post-modernist relativism. "But in the days that followed, a growing number of commentators played serious variations on the same theme: that the ideas foisted upon us by postmodern intellectuals have weakened the country's resolve.") "Postmodernism" was henceforth to be replaced by "moral clarity," and those who persisted in the decadent insistence that the one did not necessarily cancel out the other would be subjected to what William J. Bennett would call—in *Why We Fight: Moral Clarity and the War on Terrorism*—"a vast relearning," "the reinstatement of a thorough and honest study of our history, undistorted by the lens of political correctness and pseudosophisticated relativism."

I found in New York, in other words, that the entire event had been seized—even as the less nimble among us were still trying to assimilate it—to stake new ground in old domestic wars. There was the frequent deployment of the phrase "the Blame America Firsters," or "the Blame America First crowd," the wearying enthusiasm for excoriating anyone who suggested that it could be useful to bring at least a minimal degree of historical reference to bear on the event. There was the adroit introduction of convenient straw men. There was Christopher Hitchens, engaging in a dialogue with Noam Chomsky, giving himself the opportunity to generalize whatever got said into "the liberal-left tendency to 'rationalize' the aggression of September 11." There was Donald Kagan at Yale, dismissing his colleague Paul Kennedy as "a classic case of blaming the victim," because the latter had asked his students to try to imagine what resentments they might harbor if America were small and the world dominated by a unified Arab-Muslim state. There was Andrew Sullivan, warning on his Web site that while the American heartland was ready for war, the "decadent left in its enclaves on the coasts" could well mount "what amounts to a fifth column."

There was the open season on Susan Sontag—on a single page of a single issue of *The Weekly Standard* that October she was accused of "unusual stupidity," of "moral vacuity," and of "sheer tastelessness"—all for three paragraphs in which she said, in closing, that "a few shreds of historical awareness might help us understand what has just happened, and what may continue to happen"; in other words that events have histories, political life has consequences, and the people who led this country and the people who wrote and spoke about the way this country was led were guilty of trying to infantilize its citizens if they continued to pretend otherwise.

Inquiry into the nature of the enemy we faced, in other words, was to be interpreted as sympathy for that enemy. The final allowable word on those who attacked us was to be that they were "evildoers," or "wrongdoers," peculiar constructions that served to suggest that those who used them were transmitting messages from some ultimate authority. This was a year in which it would come to seem as if we had been plunged at one fell stroke

into a premodern world. The possibilities of the Enlightenment vanished. We had suddenly been asked to accept—
and were in fact accepting—a kind of reasoning so
extremely fragile that it might have been based on the
promised return of the cargo gods.

I recall, early on, after John Ashcroft and Condoleezza
Rice warned the networks not to air the bin Laden tapes
because he could be "passing information," heated debate
about the First Amendment implications of this warning—as if there were even any possible point to the warning, as if we had all forgotten that our enemies as well as
we lived in a world where information gets passed in
more efficient ways. A year later, we were still looking for
omens, portents, the supernatural manifestations of good
or evil. Pathetic fallacy was everywhere. The presence of
rain at a memorial for fallen firefighters was gravely
reported as evidence that "even the sky cried." The presence of wind during a memorial at the site was interpreted as another such sign, the spirit of the dead rising
up from the dust.

This was a year when Rear Admiral John Stufflebeem,
deputy director of operations for the Joint Chiefs of Staff,
would say at a Pentagon briefing that he had been "a bit
surprised" by the disinclination of the Taliban to accept
the "inevitability" of their own defeat. It seemed that
Admiral Stufflebeem, along with many other people in
Washington, had expected the Taliban to just give up.
"The more that I look into it," he said at this briefing,
"and study it from the Taliban perspective, they don't see

the world the same way we do." It was a year when the publisher of *The Sacramento Bee,* speaking at the midyear commencement of California State University, Sacramento, would be forced off the stage of the Arco Arena for suggesting that because of the "validity" and "need" for increased security we would be called upon to examine to what degree we might be "willing to compromise our civil liberties in the name of security." Here was the local verdict on this aborted speech, as expressed in one of many outraged letters to the editor of the *Bee:*

> It was totally and completely inappropriate for her to use this opportunity to speak about civil liberties, military tribunals, terrorist attacks, etc. She should have prepared a speech about the accomplishments that so many of us had just completed, and the future opportunities that await us.

In case you think that's a Sacramento story, it's not.

Because this was also a year when one of the student speakers at the 2002 Harvard commencement, Zayed Yasin, a twenty-two-year-old Muslim raised in a Boston suburb by his Bangladeshi father and Irish-American mother, would be caught in a swarm of protests provoked by the announced title of his talk, which was "My American Jihad." In fact the speech itself, which he had not yet delivered, fell safely within the commencement-address convention: its intention, Mr. Yasin told *The New York Times,* was to reclaim the original meaning of "jihad" as struggle on behalf of a principle, and to use it to rally his classmates in the fight against social injustice. Such use of

"jihad" was not in this country previously uncharted territory: the Democratic pollster Daniel Yankelovich had
only a few months before attempted to define the core
values that animated what he called "the American
jihad"—separation of church and state, the value placed
on diversity, and equality of opportunity. In view of the
protests, however, Mr. Yasin was encouraged by Harvard
faculty members to change his title. He did change it. He
called his talk "Of Faith and Citizenship." This mollified
some, but not all. "I don't think it belonged here today,"
one Harvard parent told *The Washington Post*. "Why bring
it up when today should be a day of joy?"

This would in fact be a year when it was to become
increasingly harder to know who was infantilizing whom.

2

California Monthly, the alumni magazine for the University of California at Berkeley, published in its November
2002 issue an interview with a member of the university's
political science faculty, Steven Weber, who is the director of the MacArthur Program on Multilateral Gover-
nance at Berkeley's Institute of International Studies and
a consultant on risk analysis to both the State Department
and such private-sector firms as Shell Oil. It so happened
that Mr. Weber was in New York on September 11, 2001,
and for the week that followed. "I spent a lot of time talking to people, watching what they were doing, and listening to what they were saying to each other," he told
the interviewer:

The first thing you noticed was in the bookstores. On September 12, the shelves were emptied of books on Islam, on American foreign policy, on Iraq, on Afghanistan. There was a substantive discussion about what it is about the nature of the American presence in the world that created a situation in which movements like al-Qaeda can thrive and prosper. I thought that was a very promising sign.

But that discussion got short-circuited. Sometime in late October, early November 2001, the tone of that discussion switched, and it became: What's wrong with the Islamic world that it failed to produce democracy, science, education, its own enlightenment, and created societies that breed terror?

The interviewer asked him what he thought had changed the discussion. "I don't know," he said, "but I will say that it's a long-term failure of the political leadership, the intelligentsia, and the media in this country that we didn't take the discussion that was forming in late September and try to move it forward in a constructive way."

I was struck by this, since it is so coincided with my own impression. Most of us saw that discussion short-circuited, and most of us have some sense of how and why it became a discussion with nowhere to go. One reason, among others, runs back sixty years, through every administration since Franklin Roosevelt's. Roosevelt was the first American president who tried to grapple with the problems inherent in securing Palestine as a Jewish state.

It was also Roosevelt who laid the groundwork for our relationship with the Saudis. There was an inherent contradiction here, and it was Roosevelt, perhaps the most adroit political animal ever made, who instinctively devised the approach adopted by the administrations that followed his: Stall. Keep the options open. Make certain promises in public, and conflicting ones in private. This was always a high-risk business, and for a while the rewards seemed commensurate: we got the oil for helping the Saudis, we got the moral credit for helping the Israelis, and, for helping both, we enjoyed the continuing business that accrued to an American defense industry significantly based on arming all sides.

Consider the range of possibilities for contradiction.

Sixty years of making promises we had no way of keeping without breaking the promises we'd already made.

Sixty years of long-term conflicting commitments, made in secret and in many cases for short-term political reasons.

Sixty years that tend to demystify the question of why we have become unable to discuss our relationship with the current government of Israel.

Whether the actions taken by that government constitute self-defense or a particularly inclusive form of self-immolation remains an open question. The question of course has a history, a background involving many complicit state and nonstate actors and going back most recently to, but by no means beginning with, the breakup of the Ottoman Empire. This open question, and its history, are discussed rationally and with considerable intellectual subtlety in Jerusalem and Tel Aviv, as anyone who reads Amos Elon or Avishai Margalit in *The New York Review* or even occasionally sees *Ha'aretz* on-line is well aware. Where the question is not discussed rationally—where in fact the question is rarely discussed at all, since so few of us are willing to see our evenings turn toxic—is in New York and Washington and in those academic venues where the attitudes and apprehensions of New York and Washington have taken hold. The president of Harvard recently warned that criticisms of the current government of Israel could be construed as "anti-Semitic in their effect if not their intent."

The very question of the US relationship with Israel, in other words, has come to be seen—at Harvard as well as in New York and Washington—as unraisable, potentially lethal, the conversational equivalent of an unclaimed bag on a bus. We take cover. We wait for the entire subject to be defused, safely insulated behind baffles of invective and counterinvective. Many opinions are expressed. Few are allowed to develop. Even fewer change.

We have come in this country to tolerate many such fixed opinions, or national pieties, each with its own baffles of invective and counterinvective, of euphemism and downright misstatement, its own screen that slides into place whenever actual discussion threatens to surface. We have, for example, allowed American biological research to fall behind that in countries where stem cell programs are not confused with "cloning" and "abortion on demand," countries, in other words, where rationality is not held hostage to the posturing of the political process. We have allowed all rhetorical stops to be pulled out on nonissues, for example when the federal appeals court's Ninth Circuit ruled the words "under God" an unconstitutional addition to the Pledge of Allegiance. The Pledge was written in 1892 by a cousin of Edward Bellamy's, Francis Bellamy, a socialist Baptist minister who the year before had been pressured to give up his church because of the socialist thrust of his sermons. The clause "under God" was added in 1954 to distinguish the United States from the atheistic Soviet Union.

"Ridiculous" was the word from the White House about the ruling declaring the clause unconstitutional. "Junk justice," Governor Pataki said. "Just nuts," Senator Daschle said. "Doesn't make good sense to me," Representative Gephardt said. There was on this point a genuinely bipartisan rush to act out the extent of the judicial insult, the affront to all Americans, the outrage to the memory of the heroes of September 11. After the June 2002 ruling, members of the House met on the Capitol steps to recite the Pledge—needless to say the "under God" version—while the Senate interrupted debate on a defense bill to pass, unanimously, a resolution condemning the Ninth Circuit decision.

These were, some of them, the same elected representatives who had been quick to locate certain upside aspects to September 11. The events could offer, it was almost immediately perceived, an entirely new frame in which to present school prayer and the constitutional amendment to ban flag burning. To the latter point, an Iowa congressman running unsuccessfully for the Senate, Greg Ganske, marked Flag Day by posting a reminder on his

Web site that his opponent, Senator Tom Harkin, who had spent five years during the Vietnam War as a Navy pilot, had in 1995 opposed the flag burning amendment. "After the tragic events of September 11," the posting read, "America has a renewed sense of patriotism and a renewed appreciation for our American flag. Unfortunately, not everyone agrees." To the school prayer point, according to *The New York Times,* a number of politicians were maximizing the moment by challenging restrictions on school prayer established by courts over the past four decades. "Post–September 11," the *Times* was told by Richard D. Land, president of the Ethics and Religious Liberty Commission of the Southern Baptist Convention, "the secularists are going to have a harder time making their case."

One footnote on the Pledge issue, and the extent to which it intersects with the case the secularists are going to have a harder time making: a significant number of Americans now recite the Pledge with another new clause, which they hope to see made permanent by legislation. After the words "with liberty and justice for all," they add "born and unborn."

All of these issues or nonissues are, as they say, just politics, markers in a game. The flag-burning amendment is just politics, the school prayer issue is just politics—a bone to the Republican base on the Christian right and a way to beat up on the judiciary, red meat for the "Reagan Democrats" or "swing voters" who are increasingly seen as the base for both parties. The prohibition on the creation of new cell lines from discarded embryos that constituted the president's "compromise" on the stem cell question is politics. The fact that Israel has become the fulcrum of our foreign policy is politics. When it comes to any one of these phenomena that we dismiss as "politics," we tend to forgive, or at least overlook, the absence of logic or sense. We tell ourselves that this is the essential give-and-take of democracy, we tell ourselves that our elected representatives are doing the necessary work of creating consensus. We try to convince ourselves that somewhere, beneath the posturing, there is a hidden logic, there are minds at work, there is someone actually thinking out the future of the country beyond the 2004 election.

These would be comforting notions were they easier to maintain. In fact we have created a political process in which "consensus" is the last thing the professionals want or need, a process that works precisely by turning the angers and fears and energy of the few—that handful of voters who can be driven by the fixed aspect of their own opinions—against the rest of the country. During the past decade—through the several years of the impeachment process and through the denouement of the 2000 election—we had seen secular democracy itself put up for grabs in this country, and the response to September 11 could not have encouraged us to think that the matter was in any way settled.

We had seen the general acquiescence in whatever was presented as imperative by the administration. We had seen the persistent suggestions that anyone who expressed reservations about detentions, say, or military tribunals, was at some level "against" America. (As in the presidential formulation "you're either with us or you're with the terrorists.") We had seen, most importantly, the insistent use of September 11 to justify the reconception of America's correct role in the world as one of initiating and waging virtually perpetual war. And we had seen, buttressing this reconception, the demand that we interpret the war in Afghanistan as a decisive victory over al-Qaeda, the Taliban, and radical fundamentalism in general.

This was despite repeated al-Qaeda-linked explosions through Southeast Asia.

Despite continuing arson and rocket attacks on girls' schools in Afghanistan.

And despite the fact that the chairman of the Joint Chiefs said in November 2002 at the Brookings Institution that we had lost momentum in Afghanistan because the Taliban and al-Qaeda had been quicker to adapt to U.S. tactics than the U.S. had been to theirs.

3

In 1988, a few weeks after George W. Bush's father was elected president, I wrote a postelection note for *The New York Review* about a trip the senior Bush had made to Israel and Jordan in 1986, when he was still vice president. He had his own camera crew with him in Israel, but not in Jordan, since, as an official explained to the *Los Angeles Times,* there was "nothing to be gained from showing him schmoozing with Arabs." Still, the Bush advance team in Amman had devoted considerable attention to crafting visuals for the traveling press. Members of the advance team had requested, for example, that the Jordanian army marching band change its uniforms from white to red. They had requested that the Jordanians, who did not have enough helicopters to transport Bush's traveling press corps, borrow the necessary helicopters to do so from the Israeli air force. In an effort to assure the color of live military action as a backdrop for the vice president, they had asked the Jordanians to stage maneuvers at a sensitive location overlooking Israel and the Golan Heights. They had asked the Jordanians to raise, over the Jordanian base there, the American flag. They had asked that Bush be photographed studying, through binoculars, "enemy territory," a shot ultimately vetoed by the State Department, since the "enemy territory" at hand was Israel. They had also asked, possibly the most arresting detail, that, at every stop on the itinerary, camels be present.

"This is in fact the kind of story we expect to hear about our elected officials," I wrote in 1988:

> We not only expect them to use other nations as changeable scrims in the theater of domestic politics but encourage them to do so. After the April 1961 failure of the Bay of Pigs, John Kennedy's approval rating was four points higher than it had been in March. After the 1965 intervention in the Dominican Republic, Lyndon Johnson's approval rating rose six points. After the 1983 invasion of Grenada, Ronald Reagan's approval rating rose four points, and what was that winter referred to in Washington as "Lebanon"—the sending of American marines into Beirut, the killing of 241, and the subsequent pullout—

was, in the afterglow of this certified success in the Caribbean, largely forgotten.

That was 1988. Fourteen years later, we were again watching the scrims being changed, but in a theater we did not own. The Middle East was not Grenada. It was not the Dominican Republic. It was not, as they used to say in Washington about the Caribbean, "our lake." It was nitroglycerin, an unstable part of the world in which we had managed to make few friends and many enemies. And yet, all through the summer of 2002, the inevitability of going to war with Iraq was accepted as if predestined. The "when" had already been settled. "Time is getting short," *The New York Times* had warned us in July, "for decisions that have to be made if the goal is to take action early next year, before the presidential election cycle intrudes." That last clause bore study.

"Before the presidential election cycle intrudes." In case the priorities were still unclear.

The "why" had also been settled. The president had identified Saddam Hussein as one of the evildoers. Yes, there were questions about whether the evildoer in question had the weapons we feared he had, and yes, there were questions about whether he would use them if he did have them, and yes, there were questions about whether attacking Iraq might not in fact ensure that he would use them. But to ask those questions was sissy, *not muscular,* because the president had said we were going to do it and the president, if he were to back down, risked losing the points he got on the muscular "moral clarity" front.

"I made up my mind," he had said in April, "that Saddam needs to go." This was one of many curious, almost petulant statements offered in lieu of actually presenting a case. *I've made up my mind, I've said in speech after speech, I've made myself clear.* The repeated statements became their own reason: "Given all we have said as a leading world power about the necessity for regime change in Iraq," James R. Schlesinger, who is now a member of Richard Perle's Defense Policy Board, told *The Washington Post* in July, "our credibility would be badly damaged if that regime change did not take place."

There was of course, for better or for worse, a theory, or a fixed idea, behind these pronouncements from the president—actually not so much behind them as coinciding with them, dovetailing in a way that made it possible for many to suggest that the president was actually in on the thinking. The theory, or fixed idea, which not only predated September 11 but went back to the Reagan administration and its heady dreams of rollback, had already been employed to provide a rationale for the president's tendency to exhibit a certain truculence toward those who were not Americans. Within the theory, any such truculence could be inflated into "The Bush Doctrine," or "The New American Unilateralism." The theory was this: the collapse of the Soviet Union had opened the door to the inevitability of American preeminence, a mantel of beneficent power that all nations except rogue nations—whatever they might say on the subject—were yearning for us to assume. "We run a uniquely benign

imperium," Charles Krauthammer had written in celebration of this point in a June 2001 issue of the *Weekly
Standard*. "This is not mere self-congratulation; it is a fact
manifest in the way others welcome our power."

Given this fixed idea, as if in a dream from which there
is no waking, and given the correlative dream notion
that an American president, Ronald Reagan, had himself
caused the collapse of the Soviet Union with a specific
magical incantation, the "Evil Empire" speech, the need
to bring our force for good to bear on the Middle East
could only become an imperative. By June 2002, Jim
Hoagland was noting in *The Washington Post* that there was

> a growing acceptance at the White House of the need for
> an overwhelming US invasion force that will remain on
> the ground in Iraq for several years. The US presence will
> serve as the linchpin for democratic transformation of a
> major Arab country that can be a model for the region.
> A new Iraq would also help provide greater energy secu-
> rity for Americans.

A few weeks later in the *Post,* Michael Kelly was sketching an even rosier outcome, based on his eccentric reading of the generation now coming of age in the Middle
East as a population poised by history to see the United
States not as its enemy but as its "natural liberator." "It is
right to think that we are living in a hinge moment in history," he wrote, and then argued against those who believe
that the moment is not necessarily ours to control. "But
it is wrong to think that the large forces of this moment
act on the hinge to shut the door against American inter-

ests." The contrary may be true, he wrote, if only we take the next step, which is "to destroy the regime of Saddam Hussein and liberate the people of Iraq." This will be, he said, "when history really begins to turn on its hinge."

It so happened that I was traveling around the country again recently, talking and listening to people in St. Louis and Columbia and Philadelphia and San Diego and Los Angeles and San Francisco and Pittsburgh and Boston. I heard very few of the fixed ideas about America's correct role in the world that had come to dominate the dialogue in New York and Washington. I encountered many people who believed there was still what we had come to call a disconnect between the government and the citizens. I did not encounter conviction that going to war with Iraq would result in a democratic transformation of the Middle East. Most people seemed resigned to the prospect that we would nonetheless go to war with Iraq. Many mentioned a sense of "inevitability," or "dread." A few mentioned August 1914, and its similar sense of an irreversible drift toward something that would not work out well. Several mentioned Vietnam, and the similar bright hopefulness of those who had seen yet another part of the world as a blackboard on which to demonstrate their own superior plays. A few said that had they lost relatives on September 11, which they had not, they would be deeply angered at having those deaths cheapened by being put to use to justify this new war. They did not understand what this new war was about, but they knew it wasn't about that promising but never quite substantiated meeting in Prague between Iraqi intelligence and Mohamed Atta. They did not want to believe that it was about oil. Nor did they want to believe that it was about domestic politics. If I had to characterize a common attitude among them I would call it waiting to see. At a remove.

Like most of them, I no longer remembered all the arguments and inconsistencies and downright contradictions of the summer and early fall. I did remember one thing: a sequence of reports. It was June 1 when the President announced, in a commencement address at West Point, that the United States military would henceforth act not defensively but preemptively against terrorists and hostile states in possession of chemical, biological, or nuclear weapons. It was June 6 when the secretary of state advised NATO in Brussels that NATO could no longer wait for "absolute proof" of such possession before taking action. It was June 10 when Thomas E. Ricks and Vernon Loeb reported in *The Washington Post* that under this new doctrine, according to Pentagon officials, the United States would consider using high-yield nuclear weapons on a first-strike basis. The use of such weapons would be reserved, according to these officials, for deployment "against biological weapons that can be best destroyed by sustained exposure to the high heat of a nuclear blast." Some bunkers in Iraq, the *Post* was told by Stephen M. Younger, the director of the Defense Department's Defense Threat Reduction Agency, are in fact "so incredibly hard" that "they do require high-yield nuclear weapons."

I never saw this mentioned again. I never heard anyone refer to it. Not even during the discussions of nuclear intentions that occurred six months later, after the administration released a reminder that the U.S. reserved the right, if it or its allies were attacked with weapons of mass destruction, to respond with nuclear as well as conventional force. But let's look at where we are.

The idealists of the process are talking about the hinge of history.

And the Department of Defense was talking as early as last June about unloosing, for the first time since 1945, high-yield nuclear weapons.

In the early 1980s I happened to attend, at a Conservative Political Action conference in Washington, a session called "Rolling Back the Soviet Empire." One of the speakers that day was a kind of adventurer-slash-ideologue named Jack Wheeler, who was very much of the moment because he had always just come back from spending time with our freedom fighters in Afghanistan, also known as the mujahideen. I recall that he received a standing ovation after urging that copies of the Koran be smuggled into the Soviet Union to "stimulate an Islamic revival" and the subsequent "death of a thousand cuts." We all saw that idea come home.

After Henry

In this foray into the American cultural scene, Joan Didion covers ground from Washington to Los Angeles, from a TV producer's gargantuan "manor" to the racial battlefields of New York's criminal courts. A bracing amalgam of skepticism and sympathy, *After Henry* is proof of Didion's infallible radar for the true spirit of our age.

Current Affairs/Literature/0-679-74539-4

A Book of Common Prayer

The intertwining story of two American women in the derelict Central American nation of Boca Grande; one controls much of the country's wealth and knows all of its secrets, while the other vainly hopes to be reunited with her fugitive daughter.

Fiction/Literature/0-679-75486-5

Democracy

Inez Victor knows that the major casualty of the political life is memory. But the people around Inez have made careers out of losing track. Her senator husband wants to forget the failure of his last bid for the presidency. Her husband's handler would like the press to forget that Inez's father is a murderer. And, in 1975, the year in which much of this bitterly funny novel is set, America is doing

its best to lose track of its one-time client, the lethally hemorrhaging republic of South Vietnam.
Fiction/Literature/0-679-75485-7

The Last Thing He Wanted

In 1984 Elena McMahon walks off the presidential campaign she has been covering for a major newspaper to do a favor for her father. Elena's father does deals. And it is while acting as his agent in one such deal—a deal that shortly goes spectacularly wrong—that she finds herself on an island where tourism has been superseded by arms dealing, covert action, and assassination.
Fiction/Literature/0-679-75285-4

Miami

It is where Fidel Castro raised money to overthrow Batista and where Castro's enemies have raised armies to overthrow *him,* so far without success. It is where the Cuban exile intersects with the cynicism of U.S. foreign policy. It is a city whose skyrocketing murder rate is fueled by the cocaine trade, racial discontent, and an undeclared war on the island ninety miles to the south. *Miami* is a masterly study of immigration and exile, passion, hypocrisy, and political violence.
Current Affairs/Literature/0-679-78180-3

Political Fictions

Through the deconstruction of the sound bites and photo ops of three presidential campaigns, one presidential impeachment, and an unforgettable sex scandal, Didion reveals the mechanics of American politics. She tells us the uncomfortable truth about the way we vote, the candidates we vote for, and the people who tell us to vote for them. A disturbing portrait of the American political landscape, and essential reading on democracy.

Current Affairs/0-375-71890-7

Run River

Joan Didion's electrifying first novel is a haunting portrait of a marriage whose wrong turns and betrayals are at once absolutely idiosyncratic and a razor-sharp commentary on the history of California.

Fiction/Literature/0-679-75250-1

Salvador

In 1982, Joan Didion traveled to El Salvador at the ghastly height of its civil war. *Salvador* is an anatomy of that country's particular brand of terror—its mechanisms, rationales, and relationship to the United States. As she travels from battle fields to body dumps, Didion trains a merciless eye not only on the horror but also on the depredations and evasions of her own country's foreign policy.

Current Affairs/Literature/0-679-75183-1

VINTAGE **READERS**

Authors available in this series

Martin Amis

James Baldwin

Sandra Cisneros

Joan Didion

Richard Ford

Langston Hughes

Barry Lopez

Alice Munro

Haruki Murakami

Vladimir Nabokov

V. S. Naipaul

Oliver Sacks

Representing a wide spectrum of some of our most significant modern authors, the Vintage Readers offer an attractive, accessible selection of writing that matters.